Praise for
Free Yourself From Fears

"It has been said that the two great emotions are love and fear, and that they form the foundation for all others. Fear tends to be the source of most of the difficult feelings we experience. Learning to deal with fear is thus one of the most important life skills a person can learn.
In *Free Yourself From Fears* Joseph O'Connor provides a wealth of knowledge and tools to help people better understand their fears and transform them into positive actions. As with his previous books, Joseph demonstrates his great gift for presenting rich and complex knowledge in a form that is both practical and easy to understand.
I highly recommend this book for anyone who wants to move more easily and confidently through life."
ROBERT DILTS, AUTHOR OF *FROM COACH TO AWAKENER*
& *CHANGING BELIEF SYSTEMS WITH* NLP

"This book is an excellent example of Joseph O'Connor's elegant, enriched writing style and conveys pertinent, powerful learning for dealing with the fears of the volatile world in which we live today."
SUE KNIGHT, AUTHOR OF *NLP AT WORK*

"With uncommon knowledge and authority, *Free Yourself From Fears* gives us a fresh view on our everyday anxieties. In plain language O'Connor combines the analytical with the intuitive and does it with heart. Therapists, managers and communicators in all fields will use his practical exercises for dealing with fear for years to come."
MICHAEL COLGRASS, PULITZER PRIZE-WINNING COMPOSER AND NLP TRAINER

Free Yourself From Fears

To Andrea

Free Yourself From Fears

Overcoming Anxiety and Living Without Worry

Joseph O'Connor

NICHOLAS   BREALEY
PUBLISHING

LONDON • BOSTON

First published by
Nicholas Brealey Publishing in 2005

3–5 Spafield Street
Clerkenwell, London
EC1R 4QB, UK
Tel: +44 (0)20 7239 0360
Fax: +44 (0)20 7239 0370

100 City Hall Plaza, Suite 501
Boston
MA 02108, USA
Tel: (888) BREALEY
Fax: (617) 523 3708

http://www.nbrealey-books.com
http://www.lambentdobrasil.com

© Joseph O'Connor 2005

ISBN 1-85788-360-8

British Library Cataloguing in Publication Data
A catalogue record for this book is available from the
British Library.

Printed in Finland by WS Bookwell.

Contents

Introduction

ON THE AFTERNOON OF SEPTEMBER 11TH, 2001, I was in England, sitting in a comfortable chair reading the paper. Suddenly my daughter ran into the room, saying she had heard on the radio that the World Trade Center in New York had collapsed. This sounded so strange, I thought she must have made a mistake, and I turned on the television to see what was happening.

The television was full of images that are now part of the nightmares of our collective unconscious. The television endlessly replayed the horrifying airplane crashes, ensuring that they were etched indelibly on everyone's minds. I felt like I was inside a bad dream, or had entered a parallel universe where the rules of life did not apply any more. It was unbelievable; I must have stared at the television for half an hour, unable to leave, and I was afraid. Then I went away and cried.

The next day I woke up hoping that it really had been a bad dream. It felt like one, one of those times when you wake up feeling relief that of course it was just a dream, how could it have seemed so convincing. And yet the tragedy really happened. For the next couple of days, life was not quite as solid as usual. I felt unreal, as if my head were slightly detached from my body. I needed a little extra concentration to understand what people were saying to me, and a lot of what people said to me didn't seem to make sense. I was dissociated, suffering from mild shock.

After a week, I looked back on the experience and wondered. How many times did the television news show those ghastly pictures of the World Trade Center towers collapsing? How many times did the media replay that appalling, yet mesmerizing, video of the second plane scything into the tower and burying itself deep in the structure like some huge knife? I don't know. I decided not to watch the collapse of the towers again on the news, and one viewing of the video was enough for me. I will not forget it. This is how fears are made. With the best of intentions, and probably feeling that they had no choice, the news media ground these images into our collective psyche like grit deep into an open wound, with a thoroughness that made them impossible to forget.

A traumatic image repeated so many times can burn its way into the mind and have an effect long after the rubble has been cleared away. The constant replaying ensured that we all took the image of the toppled towers into the future with us and this image said: you are not as secure as you thought you were. Suddenly, the world was less safe.

Those events were real and terrible, and we don't want to forget them. The consequences will follow us far into the future. Yet *how* we remember them is important. The people who flew the airplanes and those who prepared them to do so killed thousands of people and destroyed buildings. It would be worse if they destroyed our peace of mind too.

Every innocent passenger in those airplanes and every innocent person killed in the attacks is a personal tragedy, a thread in the whole ghastly tapestry of terror, each one immediate and appalling. The nature of what happened made many people fearful of flying (demand for air travel dropped dramatically after September 11th; some airline companies collapsed, nearly all had difficulties). It made us fearful of tall buildings (the price of high-rise apartments dropped radically). It made some people afraid of Muslims. And many must have looked at their children sleeping and wondered what sort of world they would inherit.

This tells us a lot about fear. Something awful happens and we are afraid of what might happen in the future and afraid of putting ourselves in any similar situation.

Freeing yourself from fears

This book is about fear and how to be free from it. Fear comes in two very different flavors, unreal and authentic.

Unreal fear comes from our creative brain making up frightening scenarios that have not happened and probably will not happen. My first goal for this book is to give you clear and practical patterns to get rid of unreal fears and worry.

There is also an insidious type of unreal fear that I am calling "social fear." This is a kind of free-floating anxiety. We are more anxious now; there is more to be anxious about. The world has become a more dangerous place, and the danger is closer to home.

While our popular culture of achievement and goal orientation has many benefits, it has drawbacks as well. We often feel that if we do not succeed, if we do not attain our dreams, if we do not have unlimited power and kick-ass self-esteem, there is something wrong—with us. We have failed. A general feeling of anxiety floats like a ghost in the wind and few escape its cold touch.

My second goal in this book is to get a better perspective on this miasma of cultural anxiety that disturbs our peace of mind, our sleep, and our digestion, and to propose some healthy antidotes.

Authentic fear is a protective emotion. It is always in response to true danger in the present moment. My third goal for this book is for you to use authentic fear as a signal to keep you safe.

This is a practical book. As well as offering some specific antidotes to limiting fears, it will also improve the quality of your life, and this is my fourth goal. When you are free of unnecessary fear you will have an emotional freedom and sense of wellbeing that will resonate throughout your life. You will be able to get your life in focus and brush aside obstacles.

This is a much more *personal* personal development book than any of my previous work. In a book on emotions and personal development, the writer needs to be in the book too. So you will find many of my personal experiences described here, especially about moving from England to Brazil.

NLP

I am using many insights from Neuro-Linguistic Programming (NLP) in this book. NLP was created by John Grinder and Richard Bandler in America in the mid-1970s and it explores subjective experience— what we think and feel from the inside. How do we do what we do? How is it that some people are exceptionally skillful and talented while others, who seem to have the same knowledge and make the same actions, get only average results? NLP was originally used to model exceptional people to find out what they were doing differently, so that these skills could be taught to others. From modeling excellence, it is a small step to model how we do anything. How do we create fear? How do we learn to be afraid? How is it that some people are afraid and others are not? Because they have *learned* to be. This does not make fear any the less real or frightening for the person who is feeling it. However, once we know how fear is created, then we have the key to free ourselves from it. NLP will allow you to unlearn your fears and free yourself from them.

You do not need any training in NLP to enjoy and use the book. You will find the NLP concepts you need explained throughout the book when you need them. More general NLP reference material is at the end.

How the book is structured

Part I deals with fear—the two types of fear, where they come from, how they are generated, how we learn them and talk about them.

Part II gives immediate practical tools to free you from unreal fear. A fear can be about the future, like the anticipation of a public speaking engagement that makes you feel increasingly uneasy as the fateful day approaches. Or it can be about the past, like a traumatic memory or flashback that makes you feel fearful in the present, restricts your life, and makes it difficult to be spontaneous. There are specific techniques to deal with many such common fears.

There are two chapters on social fears, how they come about, and what to do about them. These give you ways to deal with the worry, stress, and free-floating anxiety that come from everyday living. There is a chapter on change—how to deal with the fears that can stop you making the changes you want in your life. Many times we want or need to take a step, but are afraid to leave the comfort of the habits we know. This chapter tells you how to start the change and manage the transition—that scary in-between time when you have neither what you had before, nor what you want. You are in the middle of the journey and cannot go back.

Part III deals with authentic fear: fear as a signal to keep you out of danger and take action, and how to distinguish authentic fear from unreal fear. This section will fine-tune your intuition, so that you will know for sure when you are in danger and avoid it. It will help to make fear a reliable friend who gives you fair warning, and not a garrulous bore who is forever crying wolf. This part also shows you how to recognize when other people represent a real danger. There is a chapter on how to use trust and intuition to stay safe, and one on how to evaluate risk.

Part IV is a summing-up and an explanation of how you can use the value behind your fear to combat it. There is a chapter on controlling the unpleasant feeling so that you can be more clear-headed and resourceful, whatever happens. There are also more tools for overcoming unreal fears, both individual and social.

This book is not just about getting rid of fear. It is about enjoying the happiness and emotional freedom of a life without unreal fears.

I hope you enjoy the book, I hope it is useful. Some fears deserve to be laughed at, some deserve to be ignored, others deserve to be respected, and you need to know which is which.

The Asian tsunami happened as I was finishing this book. On December 26th, 2004, a few miles beneath the floor of the Indian Ocean, an earthquake measuring 9.3 on the Richter scale, the most powerful for 40 years, spread over 700 miles on the floor of the Indian Ocean. It created a tsunami 10 meters tall moving at 560 miles per hour that flooded huge tracts of Indonesia, Thailand, India, and

Sri Lanka, killing over 120,000 people and destroying the livelihoods of many thousands more. Once again, scientists will ask whether society should do more to prepare for such rare but catastrophic events.

It was another terrible tragedy for the people caught there, each with an individual story to tell of courage, loss, or destruction. This natural disaster and the manmade tragedy of the twin towers show us that although terrible things can happen, our spirit burns as strongly as ever, and each of us is a candle that can light other candles. Together we can create a heat and a light that can hold the darkness from the door. We owe it to ourselves to do the best we can, to make our light as bright and as clear as possible. If this book can contribute to that in any way, then I will be happy.

Acknowledgments

To my partner, Andrea Lages, I owe more than I can say. She has supported me in every way and helped me through difficult transitions and many fears. I also want to pay my usual respects to Richard Bandler and John Grinder as the co-creators of NLP. Also to my editor Nicholas Brealey, who helped me think the book through and improve it right up to the final draft. The music I especially enjoyed and was most likely to be playing while I wrote this book was by Mana ("Mulher de San Blas," one of the saddest songs ever written), Santana (*Shaman*), Antonio Jobim, Robbie Williams, Damien Rice, and Sarah McLaughlan.

Joseph O'Connor
São Paulo, February 2005

PART I

Our Experience of Fear

The nine laws of fear

1 Fear is a basic human emotion that has evolved to protect us.

2 Fear is a reaction to a mixture of a real outside event or trigger and the meaning we make of it in our imagination.

3 Behind all fear is a fear of losing something we value.

4 There are two types of fear: authentic and unreal. Authentic fear is a natural reaction to real and present danger. Unreal fear comes from our imagination.

5 The feeling of fear is always real—whatever provokes it.

6 All fear has a positive intention.

7 We are born with two basic fears: falling and abandonment. We learn other fears by:

—Example.
—Trauma.
—Repetition.
—Information.

8 Fear can be enjoyable if:

—We believe that the situation is safe.
—We feel confident that there is no real danger.
—We know that the situation will end at a definite time.

9 We can talk ourselves into feeling afraid.

CHAPTER 1

What Is Fear?

Fear is that little darkroom where negatives are developed.
MICHAEL PRITCHARD

WHAT DO WE MEAN BY FEAR? What does it mean to be afraid? Fear is a basic emotion that protects us. Fear is undeniable, that unpleasant sensation that arises when we think we are in danger. The danger may be real or imaginary. The word "fear" comes from the old English root *fer* or *fere*, meaning "danger," or "coming suddenly upon." It is interesting that the root of the word suggests there is danger that we are not prepared for. If we are prepared, then we may not feel afraid.

The word "fear" itself is an abstraction. The feeling comes from a process in the body that is triggered by something we see, hear, feel, touch, taste, or smell. And these sights, sounds, and feelings can arise from the outside world or from our imagination. Whatever the origin, fear is not something we have, but something we do.

The first law of fear:

Fear is a basic human emotion that has evolved to protect us.

Fear is not a pleasant emotion. It can range from a mild apprehension to a gut-wrenching, heart-pumping jolt that rises like a fiery volcanic eruption before congealing in the pit of the stomach like cooling lava. It rises immediately when we hear a bump in the night, or see an open window that we didn't leave open. It can ambush us and make us act without thinking. You may be happily relaxing when you suddenly realize that you left your private computer files in plain view at the office—before you know it, you have risen half out of your chair. Fear can also sneak up gradually, for example as that long-deferred visit to the dentist gets closer and closer, or that public speaking engagement that you agreed to in a moment of madness creeps up the calendar toward you like a snake.

As a rule, the more immediate the perceived danger, the more sharp, unpleasant and compelling the fear becomes. We move immediately. We act!

The two elements of fear

All fear has two elements. The first is a stimulus from the outside world. The second is the meaning we make of that stimulus and the imaginings we create about it.

The second law of fear:

The feeling of fear is a reaction to the mixture of:

1 A real outside event that acts as a trigger.

2 The meaning we make of it in our imagination.

These two elements can combine in myriad ways. Here are some examples.

The power of gravity

Imagine for a moment that you are walking alone in the country, thinking about nothing in particular. Dusk is falling and you almost stumble into a deep pit. You pull back just in time, jolted back to the present moment, your heart thumping. It all happens in half a second. The outside stimuli were the pit and your stumble; you feel frightened, you were suddenly in danger of falling, perhaps of hurting yourself badly. Falling is an archetypal fear from infancy.

This is authentic fear. It is about a real, immediate danger and about something in the present moment. It is very useful: it saves you from immediate danger and possible injury.

You know the power of gravity, so you do not think twice: your body makes a decision to pull back before you are consciously aware of it. You do not wait, balancing with your foot poised over the blackness, intellectually debating the possibility of whether it is a good idea to fall down the hole or not—you act immediately. The imaginings come *after* you have taken action to avoid the danger. They usually follow too quickly to dwell on in detail—images of you falling into the blackness and hurting yourself. The meaning is: "Danger! Take care!" After that come other thoughts: perhaps you resolve to pay more attention to where you are going when you walk in unfamiliar country in the dark. Then you may get angry that someone left a dangerous pit uncovered without a warning sign. Anger and fear are close relatives. In this example you stumble into danger, but you stay safe. The fear comes from the immediate stimulus and only after that from your imaginings of what might have happened.

A deserted alley

Here is another example. You are walking down a dark alley late at night when you hear footsteps behind you. You take a quick look around and see a powerfully built stranger swathed in a large black coat gaining on you with long strides. His face is partially hidden in the shadows.

You quicken your pace. But so, it seems, does he.

Now you start to feel apprehensive, you wonder why you are walking down a dark, deserted alley late at night. The alternative route is longer but better lit and more frequently used.

Thoughts run swiftly through your mind as you briefly debate the possible scenarios.

"I was stupid. How far is the other end of the alley? ... If I started running now would I make it? ... Suppose I started yelling? ... That's stupid. ... He's just someone walking down the alley going home like me. ... Then why is he speeding up when I do? ... Have I got anything that I could use as a weapon?"

You cross the road.

So does he.

Then you run.

That is a real situation in the present moment. Nothing has happened, but the situation is potentially dangerous. The fear makes you run, you weigh up the evidence and decide to take action. Better to look stupid than to get hurt. This fear is genuine, it happens in the present moment: there may not be real danger but you don't wait to find out. The fear is a mixture of the stimulus and your imaginings about it. If the stranger attacked you, then the fear would be strong, immediate, and authentic.

How do you decide if a situation is truly dangerous? Are you running from a real danger, or from a fantasy of what might happen? You may never know, and it is often safer that way. In this example the fear is useful: it makes you take action to get away from a potentially dangerous situation.

The parachute jump

Now a third circumstance. You decide to do a sponsored parachute jump to raise money for charity. You take the training, learn how to fall, discover how to operate the parachute (safely on the ground), and are excited about the whole idea. You and your companions feel a bond of friendship; you are all willing to put yourselves in danger to raise money for charity.

The fateful day approaches. You do not sleep so well the night before and wake up excited. Your apprehension grows as you travel to the airfield: maybe part of you hopes the car will break down or the plane will not be able to fly because of bad weather. You get on the airplane and watch the ground recede. If in the past you have been afraid of flying, this day you are not—now you are afraid of leaving the safety of the airplane. Of course, you laugh and joke and do not let people know what you are feeling.

At 7,000 feet up you get ready to jump, it's your turn. You are terrified. Why? Because your imagination has constructed all sorts of scenarios ranging from falling to the ground like a stone if your parachute does not open, to breaking a leg when you land awkwardly, or drifting out to sea. You have never jumped out of an airplane before and now it seems like a crazy thing to do. However, you trust your training. You trust your instructor. You feel confident that you know what to do. You believe that parachutes work and that the odds against yours not working are very, very small. It is important to make the jump because you have been sponsored by many friends and relatives for a large amount of money. And of course your sense of pride won't let you back out now. So you take a deep breath, commend your soul to your God, and jump...

The parachute opens, of course.

A few minutes later, you are safely on the ground feeling wonderful, all fears forgotten.

In this example, most of your fear comes before the jump, because of your imaginings of what might happen. Your fear is not about what is happening, but what might happen. It comes mostly from your imagination.

The jump could be dangerous. Parachuting is a dangerous sport and people are hurt and occasionally killed, so your fears are not groundless. However, you have the resources and the training and you believe it is possible to jump safely. Your values (raising money for charity and your pride) support you in going ahead. So while there is a small risk of danger, you believe you can handle it and you will be safe. The fear comes from your imagining of worst-case scenarios.

As you jump, the feeling is an adrenaline rush of excitement that is sometimes difficult to separate from fear. (If you pulled the release cord as you fell and the parachute did not open, then you would experience strong, authentic fear in that moment!)

The pay raise

A fourth example: A junior manager has been with his company a year and decides he needs a raise in salary. His work has been good.

His wife is pregnant. They need extra money for their child. He must ask his boss for an increase. His boss is demanding, sarcastic, and not easy to talk to. He is also known to be unsympathetic to requests for a higher salary and he can be very unpleasant if he does not like you. Our junior manager knows this and is frightened: frightened of rejection, frightened of being shouted at, frightened that he will not get the raise. None of these things has happened—yet—but his imagination makes them real. They are all imaginary scenarios, constructed in his mind as he tosses and turns in bed the night before, trying to get a good night's sleep to be ready for the day of the fateful meeting.

This is an example of unreal fear. The manager fears a future that exists only in his mind, like the parachutist in the last example, but in this case the danger is not to his life or health (his boss is not going to attack him), but to his values, self-esteem, and pride. His fear is about what might happen, not what has happened. He does not know what will happen, but the result is important to him—and his imagination rises up to fill the void.

He will feel afraid immediately before and during the meeting, and this may make him less effective at persuading his boss to give him the raise. So his fear may bring about his worst imagining. All he can do is prepare as best he can with all the facts and persuasive arguments that he can muster. He also needs to make sure he is in a good emotional state. If he did not care about getting the raise, then he would not be frightened. He cares about the raise because he cares about his family. There is an important value behind this fear.

Fear of snakes

A fifth and final example: A man with a phobia of snakes goes to watch the film *Raiders of the Lost Ark*. He is enjoying it immensely (except the scene when Indiana Jones has a snake as an unwelcome flying companion at the beginning of the film), until Indy is trapped in a pit of poisonous snakes. Then, he feels ill. He can't look. The screen is full of snakes. His mind is slithering. He can't stand it and he gets up hurriedly, pushes along the row of seats, and leaves the cinema as quickly as possible.

This is an example of unreal fear. This man is in no real and present danger. There are no snakes in the cinema. But the images are real and terrifying and have tremendous meaning for him. The environment has supplied a trigger for a fear that already existed and was probably built in his childhood. Perhaps he had a very frightening experience with a snake when he was young and has never forgotten it.

These examples show how two elements combine to create fear. Sometimes the fear comes completely from the stimulus in the present moment. Sometimes it comes completely from our imagination about what might happen. Most fear is a mixture of the two.

What these examples have in common is fear of loss: loss of life, loss of health, loss of something you value, loss of wellbeing, loss of self-esteem. Loss is a fundamental driver of fear.

The third law of fear:

Behind all fear is a fear of losing something we value.

The NLP approach to fear

NLP is about how we create our experiences and how we represent them in our minds, in our bodies, and in words.

The *neuro* of neuro-linguistic programming is about the mind, how we think. We use our senses to experience the external world and then we use our senses on the inside to think about it. In NLP terms, thinking is using our five senses internally. We see mental pictures, hear sounds and voices in our minds, create feelings, and imagine smells and tastes. These may be remembered or imagined.

NLP explores the meaning we make of the fear stimulus. It is not what we think, but how we think it that creates fear. How else can we explain why some people are afraid of heights or dogs or lifts and other people are not?

For example, one man may be afraid of dogs because when he thinks of dogs, the picture that comes to mind is a huge, slavering, growling, "Hound of the Baskervilles"-type mastiff. He may not be conscious of this image, but he knows that he is afraid of dogs. The mental picture itself may have been formed when he was a child, when he encountered a big, fierce dog, and he has never forgotten it. The good news is that with NLP, he does not have to go back to the initial traumatic event and relive it, or even remember it. With NLP he can learn to make another representation of a dog and so feel more comfortable.

We can apply the same principle to dealing with any fear with NLP. NLP suggests that we learn our fears—from experiences, from our parents and friends, and from wrong information—and helps us to unlearn them. NLP proposes that we use mental strategies; that is, how we sequence our thoughts. Unreal fear, worry, and anxiety are created by the way we think, not what we think about. This book contains many techniques from NLP to unlearn our fear strategies and to learn new ones that do not create fear.

Anchors

In common with most other psychological models, NLP also proposes that our past influences our feelings in the present. It uses the concept of "anchors." An anchor is a picture, sound, feeling, taste, or smell that automatically links to an emotional state. These anchors can be in the outside world (real sights, sounds, smells, and tastes) or in our imagination. They are formed from either unique traumatic experiences or repetition of the same experience.

Anchors are the basis of habits. They can trigger good or bad feelings. Here we are concerned with the anchors that trigger fear. With NLP we can first of all be aware of the anchors and then learn to react differently to them.

Language and physiology

The *linguistic* part of NLP deals with language. How we talk about something influences how we feel about it. Changing the language you use will change how you feel, especially as you can self-talk your self into feeling afraid.

The *programming* part of NLP is about physiology. We are all familiar with the physical feeling of fear: the tightness in our chest, the sinking feeling in the pit of the stomach. There are many ways to influence these feelings, not just to control the feeling of fear in the moment, but also to weaken the response in similar future situations—to become a calmer and less stressed person. NLP supplies ways not only to overcome fear in the moment, but also to unlearn the thinking that gave rise to fear in the first place.

The physiology of fear

Whatever the cause of fear, it always expresses itself through the body. We cannot be intellectually afraid. Fear puts us in touch with our body.

How do we create the feeling of fear? What happens? The neurophysiology of fear has been very well mapped in the last decade.

Imagine for a moment that you see a fleeting shadow outside the window and hear a suspicious sound as you sit alone watching the television one night. It could be a threat, so your neural circuits, built up over thousands of years of evolution, leap into action, much more quickly than any rational analysis.

The stimulus goes from the ear and the eye to the brain stem and then to the thalamus. From there, the nerve impulse branches. One branch leads to the temporal lobe where the visual and auditory signals will eventually be analyzed and understood. The other branch goes to the amygdala and the hippocampus. The amygdala is an almond-shaped cluster of nerve fibers just above the brain stem. The hippocampus is part of the innermost fold of the temporal lobe and is the key storage site for memories. It also analyzes the signal to compare it with other memories to determine if it is threatening or not.

If you can reassure yourself that the stimulus means nothing, then the signals stop there. If you are unsure, your brain goes to level two alert. The signal reverberates between the hippocampus, temporal lobe, and amygdala; you become more alarmed and more alert.

The amygdala is the most crucial part of this process. It is the brain's headquarters for fear. Remove the amygdala and you would not feel fear and would not be able to recognize the signs of fear in other people. The amygdala is always on the alert, sorting through your sensory impressions to see if there is anything alarming. When it is triggered, it orchestrates all the other fear reactions and feelings. It links to the hypothalamus, the part of the brain that controls movement, and to the autonomic nervous system. It signals other parts of your brain to put a frightened expression on your face and to freeze what you are doing in order to pay attention to the possible danger.

Fight or flight

The result is a "fight or flight" response that happens more quickly than conscious thought. The hypothalamus triggers the pituitary gland in the brain to produce chemicals that trigger the two adrenal glands, just above your kidneys. The adrenal glands release several hormones, primarily adrenaline, noradrenaline, and cortisol. The adrenaline produces the familiar surge in the pit of the stomach, but other changes are happening too.

The hypothalamus triggers the release of beta-endorphins, which act as painkillers so we can withstand pain and discomfort. They make us more alert. The pupils of our eyes dilate, so we see more. Our body hair stands more erect so we are more sensitive to touch, vibration, or air currents. Our hearing becomes more sensitive. The vocal chords are tightened, making our voice higher pitched. Blood flows to the large muscles where the blood vessels dilate, and away from the routine body processes like digestion. Our pulse rate and blood pressure go up. Our breathing becomes quicker and deeper to take in more oxygen to the blood for the muscles to react more strongly and quickly. We are ready for action in an instant.

When the danger is over we start to calm down, but it takes much longer for us to return to our resting state. We will be much more alert for the next few minutes. The physiology of fear and anxiety is the same as the physiology of anger; the same chemical substances are released. This explains why often people are aggressive even if the danger is averted.

For example, a mother is walking with her children, and one runs into the middle of the road in front of a car. The car stops in time and the child is safe. The mother will hug the child, but probably shout at it too. The sudden fear reaction has wired her to fight or flight and when those are blocked, this energy still needs to go somewhere.

The body responds in the same way to both unreal and authentic fear. The same chemicals are released; the body is prepared for fight or flight in the same way. The difference is that in the case of unreal fear, there is no immediate and real danger to react to. The fear response is good for immediate danger, not everyday life. When you have unreal fear, the body is left in a needless state of alert. This is a classic cause of stress. It elevates your blood pressure, disturbs your digestion, and suppresses your immune system. It impairs your thinking because blood is flowing toward the large muscles and away from the rational centers of the brain.

Some people suffer greatly from stress and anxiety. This constant stress gives rise to chronic symptoms like headaches and dizziness, blurred vision, backache, palpitations, and indigestion. Chronic stress is not good for you. It is like driving with your foot hard down on the accelerator whatever the traffic conditions. It is important for your physical health to eliminate unreal fear.

In order to explore your physical feeling of fear, you need to know your unique experience of it. NLP allows us to explore feelings in detail through submodalities, which are the smaller building blocks of our thoughts. For example, a mental picture has color, depth, and location. Sounds, either real or imagined, have pitch, volume, and rhythm. Feelings have a location and a size. These distinctions are examples of submodalities.

The next skill uses kinesthetic submodalities to explore your feeling of fear in detail. You need to know the feeling as it is now, so you can know when it decreases as a result of the techniques in this book.

Skill for freedom

How do you know you are afraid?

Think of a situation in the past when you were afraid.

Whereabouts in your body are the sensations?

How hot or cold are the feelings?

How much space do they take up?

How heavy do they seem to be?

What shape do they seem to be?

Pay attention to all your feelings.

For example, our attention is taken mostly by the feeling in the pit of the stomach, and we do not realize that the hairs on our body have become more erect (most often on the back of the neck, but in other parts of the body too).

We miss the surge of strength we feel in our body. We also can miss the increase in the rate and depth of our breathing.

Fear is much more than a bad feeling in the stomach.

CHAPTER 2

Fear—Friend or Foe?

Our doubts are traitors, and make us lose the good we oft
might win, by fearing to attempt.
WILLIAM SHAKESPEARE

THERE ARE TWO TYPES OF FEAR, authentic fear and real fear. *Authentic* fear is stimulated in the present moment by immediate danger. It spurs us to take action to avoid the danger. It is an important natural response and its intention is to keep us safe. Authentic fear is useful.

Unreal fear is stimulated by our imagining of what might happen. It is usually about something we do not want to happen in the future. It has the same positive intention—to keep us safe. It is not useful, however, except insofar as it can motivate us to take action to avoid the future scenario or to make it less likely. Sometimes unreal fear is more a vague apprehension, or a generalized anxiety because we are not completely aware of the situation we are imagining.

When a situation evokes authentic fear we will always have some thoughts and imaginings about it, but they come afterward. Authentic fear is stronger, sharper, and cuts deeper than unreal fear.

The fourth law of fear:

There are two types of fear: authentic and unreal. Authentic fear is a natural reaction to present danger. Unreal fear comes from our imagination.

The visceral feeling of fear is equally real and immediate whether it is authentic or unreal. It makes no difference whether it is a reaction to real events or imaginary events. Both feelings are real. Our brain does not distinguish between the two. We know this because when we are asleep, we can have intensely frightening dreams that are completely within our imagination.

The fifth law of fear:

The feeling of fear is always real—whatever provokes it.

Positive intention

Both types of fear have a positive intention. In other words, they are trying to accomplish something of value. Authentic fear is a strong reaction that has been built up through evolution. Its purpose is to keep us safe. The feeling is unpleasant and this provides a powerful motivation to do something about it. Our mind and body get prepared to counter any threat through fight or flight.

Unreal fear is also trying accomplish something, it is usually trying to protect us, make us pay attention, alert us to something wrong, or make us analyze the situation. However, it is not doing it in a useful way. We create the danger through our imagination and then we create unreal fear as a response. While this book is about freedom from unreal fear, we need to respect the positive intention of the fear. There are many better ways to be safe, analyze the situation, and be alert than creating unreal fear.

The sixth law of fear:

All fear has a positive intention.

Authentic fear

Authentic fear alerts us to sudden danger. It is evolution's way of saying: "Be careful!" It feels unpleasant, but has the positive intention of keeping us safe, secure, and alive. We usually learn from real fear, to avoid future danger or to find ways of coping with immediate danger.

Authentic fear can be a problem if it causes you to freeze instead of run or fight, although often your intellect does not have time to interfere and you do the right thing automatically. You may experience authentic fear when there is no real danger. For example, you are walking on the street and you see a shadow that makes you think something is falling on you. You feel fear and jump out the way. In fact it was nothing, just a shadow across the sun. However, the fear was genuine, because you believed in the moment that there was a real danger. This is about your *perception* of an event. If you went along the street fearful that something might drop on you, then this would be unreal fear.

We do not want authentic fear to paralyze us like a rabbit caught in a car's headlights. We want to take action and stop the danger. We will deal with authentic fear, how it works, and how to use it to keep yourself safe in Part III of this book.

Authentic fear

Comes from immediate danger in the present.

Keeps us safe.

Is a natural reaction to the situation.

Is a useful reaction to the situation.

We learn from it.

Stimulates us to take immediate action, although it can paralyze.

It is not always clear when there is real danger. It sometimes needs analysis.

Unreal fear

Unreal fear is a problem. It can paralyze us, make us feel less resourceful, and cannot be argued with, because it is based on imagination and not reason.

Imagination is stronger than reason. For example, imagine biting into a juicy lemon. Feel the fruit on your tongue; imagine the smell and the color in your hand. Your reason says the lemon is not there, so why are you salivating? Our mind conjures up a lemon real enough to evoke saliva, and it can conjure up imaginary scenarios that are real enough to evoke fear.

Often unreal fear is not about what has happened (past) or is happening (present), it is about what could happen (future) but has not. Uncertainty is disturbing. Without information, we fill the void with imaginings, and these are what frighten us.

Our imaginings are as lurid and frightening as the worst reality. Logic does not help. Many people are frightened of traveling by airplane. Air travel is statistically one of the safest forms of travel. But if we are frightened of flying, statistics will not reassure us. Statistics are about other people, not about us. Logic is in the service of emotion and can justify anything. Logic can be used to make any conclusion reasonable. "Don't be silly," says a well-meaning friend. "Air crashes hardly ever happen. This airline hasn't had a major crash in 20 years."

"Oh," we may think, "I'd better not use that airline, sounds like it's due an accident soon."

Unreal fear

Does not come from immediate danger, is usually a response to our imaginings of possible unpleasant futures.

Is not about the present moment.

The danger is not immediate.

Is not useful, makes us less resourceful.

Is a learned reaction to the situation.

We learn little or nothing from it.

Limits our life.

Always has a positive intention.

Types of unreal fear

There are different types of unreal fear. They range from the very intense feeling of a phobia or panic attack, through anxiety to worry. There are also social anxieties that come from the pressures of living, especially in a fast-paced, achievement-oriented society.

Phobias

What is a phobia? The word comes from the Greek *phobos*, meaning "fear," but a phobia is more than an ordinary fear. It is a sudden, irrational, and overwhelming fear about a situation, animal, or thing that is not immediately threatening. Common phobias are of snakes, spiders, enclosed spaces, and heights. Someone with a phobia cannot argue themselves out of it. They feel compelled to avoid the source of the phobia. If they cannot, they are so fearful that they have to remove themselves immediately from whatever is causing their fear.

A phobia is not fear of a real threat; the situation or animal that a person is phobic about does not pose a serious threat. Someone with a snake phobia would not be fearful because a snake was poisonous, but because it was a snake. People with a severe phobia may even be uncomfortable thinking about the situation, reading about it, or seeing pictures or films about it. Some people are phobic about flying, wide-open spaces, or being enclosed. Other common phobias are of lifts, dentists, and crowds. All these might conceivably be dangerous, but with a phobia you just avoid it and avoid thinking about it.

Phobias range from mild to intense. For example, many people are mildly phobic of heights and can't go near the edge if they are on top of a building. Some would find it difficult even to look out the window of a tall building. People with an intense phobia of heights would not risk going into a tall building in case they had to look down. The thought would be uncomfortable. If by some chance they were to be high up, they might have a panic attack and try to get down to ground level.

Someone with a phobia always knows they have it. They know there is no real danger, although they may try to justify their fear afterward. Phobias are not open to reason or argument. People may understand the phobia, know how it operates, even know how they acquired it, but still be unable to stop it.

In extreme cases, phobias can severely limit a person's life. For example, some people suffer from agoraphobia, or fear of open spaces. This makes it difficult to leave their house, even to go shopping. Every time they go out, they feel panicky. In the end, they just stop going out, and get someone else to go out and do everything for them. They will not have much social life and they construct their life around their phobia. This book does not deal with intense phobias, which require a specialized approach from an NLP therapist.

Mild phobias *can* be dealt with by techniques in this book.

The key points about phobias

A phobia is an intense, unreasoning fear.

It is possible to be phobic about almost anything.

The object of the phobia poses no real threat or danger.

No one learns from their phobia. They have the same response every time.

A phobia is not reasonable at the time—although the fear can be justified afterward.

A phobia is specific. The sufferer is aware of what causes the phobia.

Anxiety

Mild phobias shade into anxiety. Anxiety is fear with a blunt edge and is usually about the future. It may be linked with some specific situation, for example a coming public presentation. It can also be linked to a pleasant event if you are afraid of making a fool of yourself.

The derivation of the word "anxiety" is interesting. It comes from the Latin verb *angere*, meaning "to choke." This choking feeling is part of the physiological response to fear that happens through the amygdala. We often say that someone "choked" (usually in sport) when they lose at the last minute, and this is usually due to anxiety about winning (or losing).

Sometimes people may feel anxious for no reason they can articulate, it is just a vague feeling of fear, not attached to any situation or person.

The key points about anxiety

Anxiety is usually about a future event.

It can be about a specific situation or it can be a vague feeling, where it is hard to pin down the cause.

We can be anxious about a pleasant situation, if we fear that something could go wrong.

Anxiety may come for a good reason (e.g., having a dangerous surgical operation). It can also often come from our imagination where there is very little if any danger (e.g., air travel).

Worry

The word "worry" comes from the Old English word *wyrgan*, meaning "to strangle." So it embodies the same idea as anxiety. Both worry and anxiety do not let you breathe freely. Worry is very similar to anxiety, but usually less intense. Worry is anxiety on a treadmill: you go around and around, thinking of the same problem, getting nowhere. Worry is usually about the future, ruminating on what could happen. For example, hypochondriacs worry about their health, even though repeated doctors' visits tell them there is nothing wrong.

Parents worry about their children being out late, although nothing has happened. Parental worry comes from love—parents love their children and do not want anything to happen to them—but worry is not useful. It does not help to keep the children safe, and it makes the parents feel bad. It also makes the children feel bad. They want to go out and have a good time, they take every sensible precaution, and if parental worry becomes too strong it can strangle the child's freedom too.

We also talk about a dog "worrying" a bone, meaning biting it again and again. Worry has this repetitive quality. It is a form of self-harassment.

We will deal with worry in more detail in Part II of the book.

The key points about worry

Worry is usually fear of the future, like anxiety, but less intense.

Worry has a repetitive, circular quality; it goes over the same situation without resolving it.

You do not learn anything from worrying.

There is a lot of thinking, but no action.

Worry focuses on avoiding bad situations.

Social fears

Most unreal fears are specific and have specific remedies. Others are more general and pervasive. They come as part of the culture we live in. They are fed by the stories we read every day in the newspapers and see on television. These are "social fears." There are many examples.

We live in a society that values performance and achievement, therefore many people are anxious about their performance and whether they are able to achieve what they want. Competition is more intense; there are more people for fewer opportunities, so the price of failure is much higher. This makes many people fear for their job and increases their performance anxiety. Many people are afraid of failing, especially when there is so much help in the way of therapy and training. This can make them feel worse: to fail in spite of all the available help seems inexcusable and ungrateful.

Many people, especially young women, are anxious about their appearance. Surveys report children as young as five who are dissatisfied with their bodies. Diet and nutrition books are bestsellers. Plastic surgery is becoming accepted and, in some professions, essential.

Fear of authority is another general social fear. Regardless of our personal experience with authority figures, the power of the state increased in most European countries after September 11th. There is much more public surveillance, so people are afraid of being observed simply going about their everyday business.

There is now a huge amount of information on every topic and knowledge seems to have grown exponentially. Enter a query in an internet search engine and you will get millions of helpful (?) responses. The sheer amount of information makes many people anxious. Is there something important they need to know? Are they missing something? The knowledge must be out there. This can lead to a general anxiety that permeates everyday life. We will deal with these more diffuse types of social fears in Part II of the book.

The key points about social anxiety

Social anxiety is unspecific, it is part of the culture.

It tends to focus on:

    Performance.

    Appearance.

Authority.

Achievement.

Time pressure.

Threats to national security.

Social reactions to fears

The response to fear has two dimensions—the individual and the social. The *individual* dimension is what you feel about your fear. You may be ashamed of it. You may think it is normal.

The *social* dimension is how other people perceive the fear. Many fears are socially acceptable. People are sympathetic about fear of heights, doctors, dentists, and air travel (they may share the same anxiety). In English culture at least, there is little social stigma attached to phobias or anxiety. Sufferers are thought to be unfortunate, but not to blame. A phobia does not inconvenience other people, and is not infectious. Other conditions like depression, mood swings, or obsessive-compulsive behavior have much more social stigma attached, perhaps because they can affect the lives not only of the sufferer, but of others who know them.

How *not* to deal with fear

In this book we will give many strategies to free yourself from fear. There are other ways to deal with fear, which do not free you but instead enslave you more, until the cure is worse than the disease.

Authentic fear
First, what are bad reactions to authentic fear? Authentic fear can make you freeze completely, like an animal caught in the headlights. This is caused by the fear reaction controlled by the amygdala. The

positive intention is to stop you doing what you are doing so you can better attend to the danger. If you freeze and stay frozen, the result is the opposite of the intention. While you are frozen you can't do anything, you are helpless. You have to *move*!

It is equally bad to panic. Panic is mindless action without a purpose. If you panic you may jump out of the frying pan, into the fire—you can get into even greater danger. You need your critical faculties. You may need to *stop* and think once the immediate danger is past.

Anger is another possible reaction. I remember driving through a housing estate several months ago when suddenly three children aged about 12 shot across the road in front of me on their bicycles. This was the popular game of "chicken"—wait for a car and let it get as close as possible before riding across the front of it on your bicycle. I put the brakes on hard, but I would have been too late, if my reactions were all that stood between them and the Accident and Emergency department of the local hospital. However, they had judged it nicely. They were across to the other side of the road as I screeched to a halt a few yards further on. I was very relieved I had not injured them; at the same time, I was very angry that they had put me in that position. I shouted at them, but they just laughed and rode off. I was shaking with anger. They were in more danger of violence from me than they had been of being hit by my car.

The same chemical substances are released in fear and anger. However, anger needs to be controlled or it can lead to more trouble.

The best reaction to authentic fear is immediate action to get out of immediate danger, followed by critical evaluation and thought about the situation and what to do next—a balance of body and mind.

Unreal fear
There are similar bad reactions to unreal fear. You can freeze. This often comes out as "choking." You feel helpless, a bad result seems inevitable, there is nothing you can do. Some people learn to react to anxiety with this kind of helplessness: they become passive, and do nothing to help themselves directly. Medical research has shown that this type of reaction can make you ill (see References).

Unreal fear can also make you panic. One of the worst things about fear is that it can wipe your critical thinking. Not only do you feel bad, but your state makes it hard to think rationally to deal with the situation. This is why you need to change your emotional state and feel better, regardless of the situation. We will be exploring ways to do this in Part II.

Anger is another possible reaction to unreal fear. It can be useful if it gives you energy to take action against the fear, or you refuse to tolerate the situation any more. Most of the time, however, anger clouds your judgment when you need to think clearly.

Guilt is a potential reaction. Guilt is the feeling that you are responsible for some wrong, real or imagined. It can also come up as a feeling of obligation for not pleasing or helping others, or having negative thoughts about them. It is usually associated with harming others, but it can be about harming yourself. Guilt is a form of self-punishment and is one of the most destructive emotions. Its positive intention is to force you to make reparation for the wrong.

Closely associated with guilt is shame. Shame comes from being aware of your own inadequacy, bad actions, or stupidity. Feeling guilty or ashamed of your fear is useless. It puts another layer of bad feeling on top of the fear. This is called a "meta state" in NLP, in other words a feeling you have about another feeling. It adds another layer of feeling on top of what you have and it makes you feel worse.

Never feel ashamed or guilty about being afraid, even if other people say you should be or try to make you so. Work instead to deal with the fear. There is a good reason for it once you understand it and with NLP you can resolve it. Shame and guilt are the opposite of understanding and never help you deal with fear.

Finally, some people react to unreal fear by projection. Projection means that you attribute your own feelings to someone else to defend yourself from the feeling. For example, a man who is afraid of going out and meeting new people may project the fear onto his wife. He does not go out because he says his wife does not want to go out. In reality his wife has no such fear. When you project fear, you cannot deal with it because you think it belongs to someone else. A very good rule is when you think that someone is afraid of something, look in your own heart to see if you are as well.

Bad ways to deal with fear

Authentic fear	Unreal fear
Freeze	Feel helpless (choke)
Panic	Panic
Anger	Anger
	Guilt
	Shame
	Projection

Measure your fears

Here is a skill you can practice now. Below are some events or things that can be frightening, but do not threaten your health or wellbeing directly. Check which ones you are frightened of.

Skill for freedom

What are you afraid of?

Rate any of these that you are afraid of on a scale of 0–10.

A score of 0 means you are not afraid at all.

A score of 10 means you have a strong fear and will do your utmost to avoid the situation.

If the fear makes you avoid that situation, add another 10 points to your score at the end.

Darkness

Meeting new people

Small animals

Snakes

Elevators

Confined spaces

Heights

Being on a boat

Thunderstorms

Losing a friend or loved one

Not having enough money

Not achieving what you want

Deadlines

Public performance

Others not mentioned

Air travel

Open spaces

Spiders

Blood

Water

Making mistakes

Being underground

Driving a car or being a passenger

Nightmares

Losing money

Being caught up in a terrorist attack

Change

Commitment

Not looking your best

Score _____

Unreal fear limits our lives. Later we will be exploring many ways to be rid of unreal fear. Without it, you will have a life of emotional freedom that is joyful and fulfilling.

CHAPTER 3

Learning and Unlearning Fear

There is nothing more fearful than ignorance in action.
JOHANN WOLFGANG VON GOETHE

WE DO NOT LEARN AUTHENTIC FEAR, but unreal fear *is* learned. This means that it can be unlearned. You entered this world with only three built-in, hard-wired fears: fear of falling, fear of abandonment, and fear of sudden loud noises. That's all. You didn't think about them at the time when you were an infant, but all are reasonable.

Falling and abandonment can be fatal for a baby. Few people remember their infancy—nature seems to erase the memories while keeping the learning—but for babies, fear is an intensely uncomfortable and painful experience. There are no words, just feelings, and they use the robust defenses that nature has given them. A newborn has a gripping reflex that will support their body weight. And babies cry, a sound that is almost impossible for an adult to ignore; it is uniquely compelling to make adults answer with love and comfort. We hear in it the possibility of our own abandonment as it speaks to that basic fear buried in every adult and we hurry to quiet it.

Thunder or any loud noise retains the power to make us jump even as adults—we never lose the startle reflex (sudden tension in the shoulders, head pushed forward)—but then the feeling subsides. Some adults are afraid of thunder, but usually we do not fear loud sounds when we get older.

Anything you were not born with, you must have learned.

The seventh law of fear:

We are born with two basic fears: falling and abandonment.
We learn all other fears by:

—Example.
—Trauma.
—Repetition.
—Information.

If you doubt this, remember how we teach young children road safety. They are not afraid of cars. Adults respect cars, but are not usually afraid of them when the cars are sitting lifeless in driveways or parked at the side of the road. However, we are very careful of them when they hurtle toward us at speed. Half a ton of heavy metal can kill you even when it is traveling slowly. Cars have killed more people than lifts, spiders, flying, and snakes put together. How is it that we are able to be reasonable about cars, yet may be afraid or phobic of lifts, spiders, flying, open spaces, and many other things that pose far less danger than cars? It has something to do with familiarity and control, but this does not completely explain it.

We learn to fear many more things in our lives than abandonment and falling. Show a baby a spider and he will probably try to eat it rather than start crying. However, if his mother or other adults around him react with fear to the spider, then so will the baby. Babies and children watch adults carefully and learn most things from them without being told.

Imagine you were put into an unknown environment. You had no idea what was dangerous and what was not, but if you saw the inhabitants (who you are sure know this environment) react with fear to something, you would too. Why take the chance? This is exactly the situation young children face. Children learn by copying, by watching those large adults who seem to know so much about this complex world. We learned to be afraid: sometimes with good reason, sometimes with no reason except that others had learned to be afraid and they passed on the learning to us.

How we learn unreal fears

We learn our fears in many different ways:

❑ *By example*. Our parents or significant adults show they are afraid of something and a child learns that too.

❑ *By trauma*. A child has a bad experience and generalizes it. For example, a child goes to hospital and is treated badly. Perhaps she suffers a lot of pain. She may conclude that all hospitals and all doctors are to be feared and she may keep a fear of doctors and hospitals into adulthood. She may even forget the initial experience, but the fear remains. This is often how phobias are built, in an intense, one-time, painful experience.

❑ *By repetition*. We may have a series of bad experiences. For example, a person may have a number of upsetting experiences with authority figures, starting with his teachers. As time passes, he learns to be afraid of authority figures because he consistently has bad experiences when dealing with them. None of the experiences is traumatic, but the weight of them builds the fear.

❑ *By information*. We hear about danger and come to believe it. News stories are often the cause of this. We hear about other people's bad experiences and this makes us afraid. We avoid similar situations because we do not want to suffer in the same way. The information may be mistaken, or the circumstances may be unusual, and it does not mean that we will have the same experience, but often we do not want to find out. For example, there may be a rash of stories about the dangers of travel to Africa. People are attacked or fall ill. We may decide not to travel to Africa as a result. While the stories may be true, that does not mean these things will happen to us. There are plenty of news stories about disasters and dangers, but very few saying the dangers are over, so our learning is never brought up to date.

Children's fears

We learn our fears mostly when we are children. That is when the world can be most threatening, because we have very little control over what happens. We have to learn what is dangerous and what is not. Unfortunately, we often make mistakes and then forget we have made them. Consequently, we may have many fears that are long past their sell-by date. They might have been reasonable at the time, because we did not know better, but they have never been updated in the light of adult experience. What can children's fears tell us about learning and unlearning fear? How do unreal fears develop?

Fears at different ages

Specific fears tend to develop and be dominant at different ages. From the age of five months to ten months, infants are afraid of strangers as they begin to distinguish between those people they know and those they do not know or do not remember. Strangers are dangerous. Many adults still have this attitude—they assume that a stranger is hostile unless proved otherwise.

Toddlers suffer from separation anxiety from the age of about twelve months to eighteen months. During this time, the child may worry about being separated from a parent. This is more common if the child has recently experienced a loss or death of a relative, friend, or pet, or is undergoing a major change, such as the parents separating or the family moving house.

From the age of two to four years, the child is making sense of the world and telling the difference between fantasy and reality. They may be afraid of the dark. Parents may have to constantly reassure them that there are no monsters under the bed and check the wardrobe for monsters several times a night. When the lines between imagination and reality are blurred, logical argument does not work. The child needs to trust the parents, or have some remedy like a "magic" ray gun, to combat the monsters.

From four to six years, children are afraid of separation from parents, so they are often frightened of going to school. They may still be frightened of the dark and of getting lost. From six to eleven years, the commonest childhood fears are about being physically hurt: fears of dentists, doctors, thunder and lightning, and burglars.

After the age of twelve, the most common fears are about social situations, taking tests, giving public presentations, being rejected by others, being embarrassed, and being ridiculed or fooled by the opposite sex.

Helping children overcome fears

Children's fears are just as intense as adult fears. They fear many things that adults fear, and they have special fears of their own. Their fears can be dealt with in very similar ways to adult fears. People sometimes think that because children fear things that are strange or unreasonable (at least to our adult reason), their fears are less intense and less important. But fear is based on perception, not reality. It is worse for children if adults ridicule their fears. They have to cope with the fear *and* the ridicule. Sometimes they will keep fears and worries to themselves because they are ashamed of them, or do not want to trouble other people with them.

When you need to help a child with a fear, start by accepting it exactly as they describe it. You may think it is unrealistic, or mistaken, but just listen. By taking the fear seriously, you reassure the child that you take them seriously.

Secondly, give them any real information they need that is appropriate to their age, to help them evaluate the fear. Make it accurate. Do not try to persuade them out of their fear, or gloss over it. This information may not help them overcome the fear immediately. The person who gives the information is often more important than the information itself. They need to trust you. The more they trust you, the more they trust the information.

I remember when my five-year-old daughter came to me very upset and asked, "Daddy, will I have to break a bone to grow up? I don't want to. It'll hurt."

I reassured her that of course she wouldn't. I asked her where she got that idea. She told me that many adults she knew kept saying how they had broken bones in the course of growing up. She had come to the conclusion that it must be compulsory in order to become an adult. I told her that although many people had broken bones when they were young (I had broken an arm), these were accidents and there were plenty of adults who had not. The next day, I found some friends who had never broken any bones and this reassured her. She was frightened by the conclusion she had drawn from the only information she had. And of course, if she had said nothing and accepted the fear, then I am sure she would have found a way to break a bone before her teens.

Thirdly, you need to help a child take control of their fear in their own way. We know that control reduces fear. To deal with a child's fear, especially if it is about something that is real to them but not logical, offer them a solution that works for them and gives them a means of control that comes from the way that they think about the fear.

Skill for freedom

Helping children with fears

1 Help the child take control of their fear in their own way.

2 Give them the information they need, appropriate to their age.

3 Accept that the child is afraid. Do not make them feel bad about it.

4 Find a solution that works in their reality and makes sense in their world.

The dream catcher

Here's another example of helping a child with their fear. When my daughter was seven years old, she was having nightmares about monsters chasing her down endless corridors. She would wake up in the middle of the night, very frightened, and have trouble getting back to sleep. She had these dreams at least twice a week and after a while she became frightened of going to sleep at all, because she was afraid of the dream.

There were all sorts of possible explanations and reassurances that I might have given. "It's just a phase" would not have been helpful (although it would have reassured me). Even if it was a phase, it was an uncomfortable one, and she needed help. Children are not normally impressed by explanations and promises about a better future as a reason to tolerate a bad present. They live more in the present moment than adults. Equally, a Freudian psychodynamic explanation would probably have scared her more than the dreams. And "pull yourself together!" doesn't work for most children (and very few adults either).

That summer I had been in the USA and traveled a little in Arizona. While I was there, thinking of my daughter, I had bought her a Native American dream catcher. This is built like an oval spider's web of brightly colored strands of fabric with colored feathers attached, and ribbons of braided leather streaming down from the main oval. You hang it beside your bed before you go to sleep. The dreams that want to visit you float beside your head in the night, and they are attracted to the brightly colored dream catcher. They have to pass through it to reach the sleeper. Good dreams are like gossamer, they pass easily through the delicate web of the dream catcher. The worse the dream, the heavier, darker, and bigger it is. These bad dreams are trapped in the web of the dream catcher and so cannot reach the mind of the sleeper. In the morning, you take the dream catcher and shake out the dreams that were caught, and they dissolve in the sunlight.

My daughter was delighted with her present, but skeptical at the same time. "Does it work?" was her main question. I said that I had tried it myself and did not have any bad dreams (this was true), and that it worked for many people. I said that we don't really understand what dreams are or how they come, so why not try it. It would probably work for her. My daughter was a pragmatic seven year old, so she tried it. She trusted that I wanted to help her. The dream catcher worked. We shook out the dust every morning in the sunlight; it was a good, comforting ritual.

Occasionally she would have a bad dream, so we repositioned the dream catcher over her bed, or made the web finer. After a month or so, she had no more nightmares. The dream catcher gathered dust and dreams unattended for six months before disappearing into a drawer. I would certainly not claim that the dream catcher works literally, but it made sense to my daughter: it gave her control, so it worked in practice.

Reassuring rituals work for children. A child's world is an exciting, wonderful, and sometimes frightening place, because they have less knowledge and less control than adults. With older children, many of the patterns in this book will work well.

Fears can persist after childhood

Some fears persist into adulthood when in fact they are out of date. A large survey of Chicago schoolchildren a few years ago showed that they were most afraid of lions, tigers, and snakes. Surveys in the UK come up with similar results. Polls for adults show that they are afraid of dentists, snakes, spiders, public speaking, and air travel.

The most common fears are of thunder and lightning, blood, heights, darkness, narrow confines, and social scrutiny. Thunder is a sudden loud noise and like any sudden noise makes us react involuntarily. We tense our shoulders in a characteristic way. Thunder is the archetypal sudden loud noise that makes a baby cry, so it is not surprising that the fear of thunder stays with many of us. Lightning always goes with thunder, but is more spectacular than dangerous, unless you are out unprotected in a thunderstorm.

Many people are afraid of blood and faint at the sight of it, especially women. Fainting is a useful reaction only if the blood is your own because it lowers your blood pressure and puts you flat out on the ground; both reactions cause you to lose less blood. Women often have lower blood pressure than men and so a drop in blood pressure is more likely to make them lose consciousness.

Many people are afraid of being alone and are more afraid of being alone in the dark than of being in the dark with others. The dark is not so frightening when you have a companion. This probably harks back to the infant's fear of abandonment.

Fear of heights is probably related one of our primary fears from infancy, fear of falling.

Fear of social scrutiny also links with the infant's fear of abandonment. We want to be accepted and we need human companionship. When other people are looking at you and judging you, this is usually a prelude to you being rejected.

Adults conquer these fears for two main reasons. First, more years and experience make things familiar and we have more confidence in our ability to handle things. The more familiar something is, the less we are frightened of it. Secondly, we have more control as adults; we do not feel at the mercy of unknown forces as children do.

Logically, we should now be afraid of cars, knives, electrical appliances near baths and showers, power drills, and chain saws, rather than the venemous snakes and spiders of which our ancestors were afraid. Cars kill hundreds of thousands of people worldwide— drivers, passengers, and pedestrians. They are mundane and familiar, but that does not make them any the less dangerous. We are careful about them, but they do not inspire fear in the way that a snake does. Snakes and spiders kill very few people. Why be afraid of them now?

I am not suggesting that we add a host of new, modern fears to the ones we already have. But it is clear that many fears are no longer as useful as they were, yet we retain them.

The modern dangers have not had a long evolutionary timespan to insinuate themselves into our psyche. Thousands of people are hurt every year in accidents in the home, falling off small stepladders, hitting fingernails instead of metal nails, or stabbing themselves with screwdrivers. People die every day because of smoking cigarettes. They die of lung cancer, emphysema, and heart disease. Smokers hold onto their rights to hurt themselves, and many people have no choice but to breathe smoke from other people's cigarettes. Yet if you ran screaming from these smoldering tubes of dried vegetable strands people would think you had gone crazy.

We are not afraid of these things because they are familiar and we feel we are in control of them. When we believe we are in control, we tolerate the danger. Many people are nervous when someone else is driving, but will take more risks when they drive themselves because they feel in control. When someone else is driving, they spend the time tensing their feet and stamping on imaginary brakes.

Enjoyable fear

Can fear be enjoyable? Yes. The feeling is very like excitement. As long as we believe there is no real danger, we can enjoy being frightened.

Fear makes you feel more alive because of the extra muscle strength, the increased heart rate, and the extra sensitivity you experience. Everything is more vivid, because your senses are more acute.

One of the first games parents play with children is "peek-a-boo" or hide and seek. The parent hides and then surprises the infant. Infants love this game—as long as they know it is a game. There is the enjoyable build-up of fear, just long enough before the parent appears suddenly. If the parent leaves it too long, then the infant will get anxious and start crying.

As we get older, we find more sophisticated versions of this basic game. These games have a message: "Ha! It's only me!" In other words, we love to be frightened as long as we can also feel safe. We seek out fear and reassurance together. Many people want that sensation of fear, because it makes them feel more alive. There are multi-million-dollar industries to cater for our fears, so we can feel the sensation—safely.

Go to a local funfair or amusement park and try the rollercoasters and the spinning rides and the haunted houses. No one complains if the haunted house is too spooky, only if it is not spooky enough. Best of all, go to Disneyland or Disneyworld. The Walt Disney Corporation has made itself one of the most successful and profitable brands in the world, because it knows what the child in the adult wants and gives it to them. There are haunted houses, realistic snakes and spiders, and sudden noises, lifts that get jammed, strange and spooky noises—all the things that frighten us normally. We go to a fair or amusement park to escape from the cares of life and have a good time. And what are they full of? Childhood fears—but in safety.

The eighth law of fear:

Fear can be enjoyable if:

—We believe that the situation is safe.

—We feel confident that there is no real danger.

—We know that the situation will end at a definite time.

Rollercoasters

Think about rollercoasters. Every year, different amusement parks vie to open the most extreme rollercoaster. State-of-the-art software calculates just how much centrifugal and centripetal force a human body can tolerate and designs the ride to the limits. Theme parks try to surpass their rivals to deliver the most exciting ride. Design engineering teams spend far more time designing a rollercoaster than designing a skyscraper.

People travel the world seeking the edge of endurance, the ultimate thrill on a rollercoaster. One of the latest at the time of writing is the one at Six Flags Magic Mountain in Los Angeles, California. It is 190 ft high and drops 215 ft at its greatest elevation at an angle of 88.5 degrees. That is just 1.5 degrees off a vertical drop. It has a top speed of 76 mph and a length of over half a mile. Riders are seated in vehicles that spin independently 360 degrees forward and backward.

And what do you experience if you ride this monster? You leave the starting point traveling backward and start to ascend vertically for 190 ft. You can see where you have been, but not where you are going. (Perhaps that is just as well.) Then the car begins its near-vertical drop; just as it does so, it flips so there is nothing between you and the ground below. You begin a 215 ft drop at an angle of nearly 90 degrees and just as you reach the top speed of 76 mph, the car flips again. Then you are into an 185 ft turn, called the Raven, because it seems you are flying like a bird... There are more turns and flips before you come back to a halt, shaken and stirred and maybe wondering where you left your stomach.

There are two main reactions to reading that last paragraph. One is: "Wonderful! I'd really like to try that!" The other one (which I share) is: "Are you insane? Wild horses wouldn't get me on that!"

Fear builds up before the ride (especially if you have not been on it before). In the queue, waiting, hearing the screams of the riders eight stories above you... inching closer to the start... sitting in the car... you can't back out now... what would your friends say? Your family would tease you for the rest of the day. Anyway there's someone older/younger/bigger/smaller than you in the queue and they don't seem to be frightened. Now you are being strapped in... and it's too late to stop *nowwww*... On the ride itself, you're so full of adrenaline and into the experience that there is no room for imaginary fears or speculations. Then, after the rush, it feels good when you stop. You survived. You are still alive. These emotions are underneath all the thrills that people seek. The mundane world seems less vivid, less real. So perhaps you join the queue to ride again.

What makes this fear acceptable is the thought that you will be safe in the end. Rollercoasters *are* safe. We want to be frightened, but safely. When we are not personally in control, we want to know that someone trustworthy and reliable is in control. No one rides a rollercoaster after reading stories of structural weaknesses in rollercoasters and a summary of all the fatal accidents on them for the last few years. After theme park accidents where rides collapse, sometimes hurting or even killing people, visitor numbers to the parks go down.

Horror films

A good horror movie has its effect in a similar way. It draws you in, it must make you sympathize and identify with a character. You have to care. Then suddenly, when something happens, you are frightened. In the movie *The Shining* there is a passage where a man has come to the haunted hotel to help a little boy who is in trouble. This man seems to be the hero, so you might assume he will be safe—then the crazy character played by Jack Nicholson jumps out from behind a pillar and nearly cuts him in half with an axe. It's on film in front of you, but you still flinch.

In most horror movies, when something scary happens, there is usually a surge of loud music or a sudden metallic sound that goes with it. It adds to your fear by making you jump, tapping into the fear of sudden loud noises from childhood. Also, horror films employ camera tricks to make you think you are closer to the floor than you are. They show everyday objects from below, often in a strange light and from an unusual angle. This is designed to make you feel like a child again, because when you were a child, you were closer to the floor. Objects that are familiar now were not familiar then and there was more to be afraid of.

It feels good to be afraid when watching a horror movie because it's only a film, and in the end the monster is destroyed, the genie goes back into the bottle. It is like after a bad dream, when we wake up and breathe a sigh of relief that it was only a dream. We like to build tension in the body, even if that tension is not particularly comfortable, so that it feels good when it stops.

With rollercoasters or horror movies we seek out fear. We do this because we look ahead and put the fear into perspective. We believe everything will be all right. Any fear will be caused by uncertainty (are the cars on the rollercoaster safe?). The more we know that the situation is under control, the more we can give ourselves over to the delicious sensation of being frightened.

Unlearning fear

Freedom comes from unlearning and eliminating unreal fear.

As we have seen, we learn fear from information, repetition, trauma, and example. Nobody forgets to be afraid. How do we remember the lesson? How do the trauma and repetition stay ingrained in our mind to affect us months and years later? What happens?

NLP proposes that one of the main reasons is that the fears are "anchored" and triggered anew in the present whenever we experience the anchor. An anchor is anything that you see, hear, or feel that triggers a response or an emotional state, in this case fear. Anchors are all around us—whenever we respond without thinking, then we are responding to an anchor.

Fear is a habit

Anchors trigger habits. Think of being afraid as a habit that you can unlearn. Anything we have learned in the past and carry out without thinking in the present is a habit—and fear is no exception. We can learn to be afraid of anything—we make anchors that bring back the fear whenever we see them. Airplanes, authority figures, lifts, spiders: all can make you anxious if they are anchors and if you have learned to be afraid of them. There is nothing inherently fearful about any of these. We were not afraid of them when we were infants. If they evoke fear then it must be because we have learned it. They act as automatic triggers to the fear response.

Emotional freedom comes from being aware of the anchors you have and choosing to respond only to the ones you want.

Unlearning fear: Being aware of anchors

Be aware of the anchors you have that make you fearful. Anchors are timeless—once set up, the habit of fear runs by itself. To overcome a fear that is triggered by an anchor, you first need to become aware of the anchor and then to break it. You break it by consistently using one of the physical or mental strategies against fear that we will discuss in Part II. You stop your old response and build a new one—one that is more in tune with how you want to be and gives you more emotional freedom.

The second step is to build an anchor for a good feeling that will counteract the fear. These are called resource anchors and we will also deal with them in Part II. A resource anchor is something you see, hear, or feel that associates strongly with a good feeling you need in the situation. It will change your state so that you can think more clearly and decide what to do about the situation. My daughter's dream catcher is an example of a resource anchor.

Before we move to Part II with its specific techniques to deal with different sorts of fear, we will look at the third aspect of NLP—language, and how our words can be used to build fear as well as relieve it. This involves not just the words we speak, but the internal dialogue we have with ourselves that helps to sustain our reality of how we think the world is.

CHAPTER 4

The Language of Fear

Your immune system is always listening in on your self-talk.

DEEPAK CHOPRA

LANGUAGE IS THE *L* IN NLP. Language, thinking, and physiology are inextricably bound together. When you calm the body, it helps to disperse the mental pictures that are behind the unreal fear and you stop telling yourself and other people you are afraid. When you stop the mental pictures, you calm the body. In both cases, it affects the way you talk about fear.

Talking yourself into fear

How does language contribute to fear? First, internal dialogue can make you fearful. When you talk to yourself about how frightened you are, or how frightening some things will be, then you feel afraid. People who talk to themselves about how awful a flight will be and how unsafe airplanes are will be frightened before and during the flight. You can use your internal dialogue as a resource against fear (see opposite). That means that it can also be used to *generate* fear. A scared voice tone will make you feel scared. So, when you are fearful, talk to yourself in a calming, reassuring voice tone. Also, use positive phrases, like "I am feeling calm." Don't use negative phrases about what you do not want. So for example, do not say to yourself "Don't be afraid" or "I am not afraid," because this just draws your attention to your fear. Also use phrases in the present tense. Say "I am feeling calm" and not "I want to feel calm." Say what you want as if it is happening as you speak.

The ninth law of fear:

You can talk yourself into feeling afraid.

Skill for freedom

Using internal dialogue to calm fear

When talking to yourself about your fears:

❏ Use a calming, reassuring voice tone.

❏ Use positive sentences in the present tense. Say "I am feeling calm" rather than "Don't be afraid."

Remember that what you say to yourself is like a hypnotic suggestion, especially if you keep repeating it. Here is a personal example. When I was in my first year of secondary school, the English homework was to prepare a talk to give to the class about a film I had seen. I did the homework at the last minute; it was no more than a set of notes. The next day in the English class, everyone had to go to the front of the room and give their presentation. I hardly listened to my classmates' presentations (except to note how good they were), but was willing the time to go quickly so the class would end before it was my turn. Alas, I was not able to freeze time and my turn eventually came. It was an awful experience for me (and no doubt for the class too), as I mumbled through my notes and sat down afterward to an embarrassed silence. I can still remember the Cheshire-cat grin on the face of the English teacher.

This experience convinced me that I could not speak in public. Whenever I tried, the picture of my English teacher's grin would rise in my mind and I would feel afraid of humiliation. It was years afterward that I eventually gathered the courage and came to enjoy public speaking. It was not as awful as I feared. (And I was not 11 years old any more.)

Fearful stories we tell to ourselves are like toxic hypnotic scripts: they lie there poisoning us unless we drag them into the open to look at them in the light of new knowledge. A hypnotic command is one that compels you to act in a certain way without knowing why. The evocative quotation from Deepak Chopra at the beginning of this chapter sums it up very well. Your self-confidence and self-esteem are also listening to your internal dialogue.

Telling other people

Internal dialogue is not the only way to use language to generate fear. Speaking aloud can also work against you. If you want to overcome your unreal fears, do not tell them to other people unless there is a very good reason. When you tell other people your fears, they believe you (of course). Then they treat you as if those fears are real: they confirm you as a fearful person. They will expect you to be afraid in certain situations and this makes it very easy for you to slip into the pattern.

There is a lot of power in making something public. You can use this power by asking people to help you when you tell them your unreal fears. Then they will treat you in the way you want to be treated.

Affirmations

Affirmations are clear, short statements of something you want to happen. They should be written down and repeated regularly. You say what you want to be true. They need to be carefully phrased.

When you make affirmations about self-development, such as being free from an unreal fear, phrase them as if they are occurring now. For example, if your goal is to be a confident public speaker, then a suitable affirmation would be: "I am becoming more and more confident about public speaking." (Since confidence without competence is usually a disaster, you should add: "I am become better and better at speaking in public.")

Do not phrase any affirmation as if it has actually happened and do not give yourself a deadline. Write down your affirmations on good-quality paper in your best writing and repeat them several times a day. This is a way of demonstrating to yourself that you take them seriously. Some people even put them on the wall where they are always visible.

Is fear compulsory?

Language gives us some clues about the meaning of fear.

We say that something "makes" us afraid. How does it do that? What is the compulsion?

This is known as a *distortion* in NLP language patterns. While cause and effect may be built into the physical world where Newton's laws of motion are a fair guide to what happens, there is no such thing as Newton's laws of emotion. To say that something makes you afraid is to deny that you have a choice.

There are two ways to challenge the compulsion.

The first is to ask yourself: "How exactly does it make me afraid?" This is an opportunity to become aware of the anchor and how you learned the fear through the skills in Chapter 17 (page 215).

The second way to challenge it is to ask yourself: "Do I have a choice about being afraid?" This is an opportunity to use the calming skills in Chapter 16 (page 208).

Our relationship with fear

Whatever we say, words define our relationship to fear. For example, in English we say "I am frightened of..." In Portuguese, the phrase is *Ter medo de...*, which translates as "I have fear of..."

"To have fear" is different to "I am frightened." If you have fear, then it is a possession, not intimately connected with you, and so it can be easier to deal with. Something you *have* is something you can put down or lose. Something you *are* is harder to lose.

In English, there are many ways to express fear in words. As you try the following skills, check what the words do to your thinking and pay attention to the exact words.

Skill for freedom

Talking about fear

Take something that you are mildly afraid of (X).

Say the following phrases to describe your fear. For the best effect say them aloud. Notice how you feel about each.

"I am terrified of X."

"I am frightened of X."

"I am afraid of X."

"I am anxious about X."

"I am phobic of X."

"I am worried about X."

"I am apprehensive about X."

How do you feel about these sentences? Do any sound false? Does your feeling change along with the words?

The words we use to describe our relationship to fear are also very important.

Having and being

Think of something you are frightened of, or have been frightened of, and say to yourself: "I am frightened of (that)."

Then say: "I have a fear of (that)."

Do the two phrases give a different feeling? How do they change your relationship to your fear?

Passive and active

Now try this.

Say to yourself, "(That) frightened me." Here you are passive, being acted on.

Then say: "I am frightened of (that)." Here you are active, doing something.

Is there a difference between "I am frightened of that" and "That frightened me"? In the first the emphasis is on you. In the second the emphasis is on what frightened you. The different emphasis will change your thinking.

Present and past

Pick something that you really fear. Say to yourself: "I am afraid of (that)."

What do you feel?

Now say: "I was afraid of (that)."

Notice that the second phrase is more precise. You were afraid of it in the past. How do you feel about that?

Cause and effect

Now say to yourself: "That made me afraid."

How does that feel?

In this example, it seems like you have no choice in the matter, it was simple cause and effect.

Inside or outside

Now think about the phrase: "To live in fear." What does it imply?

It implies that fear is something like a container you are inside, it surrounds you—a very uncomfortable state.

Now think about the phrase "living with fear." Now fear is outside you. It is something like a companion, albeit an unwelcome one.

Holding and letting go

Now think about "to be in the grip of fear." Fear is outside you but it has you, you feel caught.

Another similar phrase is to be "paralyzed by fear." You cannot move emotionally or intellectually, all escape routes seem to be closed or too dangerous. It is like the fear that strikes you when you are the edge of a cliff. You can do nothing.

Now say to yourself: "I am free of fear." How do you feel about that?

Each of these phrases gives you a slightly different relationship to fear, and some may be more comfortable than others to think about. The first step in letting go of an unwelcome fear is to change the way you think about it, and one of the best ways of changing the way you think about it is to change the words you use to describe it.

Metaphor

A metaphor is a comparison and a good metaphor is worth a thousand words. The word "metaphor" comes from the Greek *metapherein*, meaning "to carry beyond." Metaphors carry us to different meanings and make us think about everyday things and feelings in a different way.

Fear can be described in many ways, but what does it mean for you? What would be your metaphor for fear?

Fill in the blanks:

Fear is like . . . .
Because . . . .

For example, fear is like:

A cold reminder of mortality.
An alarm bell for danger.
Drowning.
A sudden vision.
Cold water down the spine.
A volcano in the stomach.
Being strangled.
A mind killer.

Take a close look at your metaphor. It defines your relationship to fear.

What resource fits the metaphor? For example, if fear is like molten lava in the stomach, then a resource is something cold. If fear is like ice in the stomach, then the resource is something warm.

This metaphor can give you a valuable hint about what to do when you feel unreal fear. For example, maybe a hot drink would help if fear seems like ice.

The better you know your own unique fear feeling, the better you will be able to deal with it. The first step to conquering an enemy is to know them well, their habits, likes and dislikes, their routine. How you think of unreal fear will tell you this.

The Bene Gesserit litany

I will not fear. Fear is the mind killer. Fear is the little death that brings total obliteration. I will face my fear. I will permit it to pass over me and through me. And when it has gone past I will turn the inner eye to see its path. Where the fear has gone there will be nothing.
Only I will remain.

THE BENE GESSERIT LITANY AGAINST FEAR, FROM *DUNE* BY
FRANK HERBERT

Dune is a great book of science fiction, made into a less than great film several years ago, and then followed by some even worse sequels. Frank Herbert created a world of memorable characters, some with great power, some with great fear. One part of the world of *Dune* is the Bene Gesserit sisterhood, a powerful, fey group of women who had considerable powers of mind control, over both themselves and others. The words "Bene Gesserit" are Latin and their closest meaning is: "She would have done good." The above quote is their litany that they teach their novices. It has some interesting ideas and metaphors within it.

First, "I will not fear." Without a context, I do not think it is possible and even if it were, it would not be a good idea. Fear will arise in response to sudden danger without warning or control. Willpower comes from the conscious mind, whereas fear comes from deeper physiological processes that we have no control over. Fear is too basic and too important to be willed away, and it is not under the control of willpower. This litany only applies to unreal fear.

"Fear is the mind killer." Yes, fear can paralyze your thinking, but it can also make you act quickly and decisively. Fear, like many other emotions, makes it harder to think clearly—at just the time when you need to think most clearly and feel more resourceful.

"I will face my fear" is an interesting expression. What could it mean to face your fear? You look at it and oppose it. You do not hide from it and you do not hide from the situation that brought it on. This is courage. It may seem that courage is the ability not to feel fear. If this were so, it would not be a virtue and we would not admire it. Courage is feeling the fear and going ahead anyway.

"I will permit it to pass over me and through me." Another interesting metaphor, which separates you from the fear and makes it move. When fear moves, you cannot be paralyzed by it. If it goes through you, it must end up behind you. Then you can "turn the inner eye to see its path."

Once it has gone, only you remain. We can use these metaphors.

Skill for freedom

The Bene Gesserit process

❏ Think of something you are frightened of or worrying about. Make it something where the feeling is unpleasant, you are not sure what to do, and the feeling is getting in the way of your effective action.

❏ Imagine the situation and feel the feeling. Give it a label. It could be "fear," "fright," "anxiety," or "worry."

❏ Now imagine that feeling in front of you. Look at it. What does it look like? What color is it? Is it like a smoky cloud? Or a green gooey mass? How big is it? How solid? What does it smell like? Does it have a sound as it hovers there in front of you? Watch it carefully. Listen.

❏ Now let it stream past you. Let it go over you, under you, and around you. Let it go through you and as it does, it will become like a wisp of smoke.

❑ As it streams around and through you, it will go behind you. Imagine that you can see it behind you disappearing faster and faster into the distance, until it melts into nothingness, as if it is being sucked down one of those enormous wind tunnels. There is nothing left. If you feel a little residue of the feeling, just put it in front of you again, face it, and repeat the process.

❑ Now feel your body solid and grounded. You remain. You are not this feeling, because you can separate yourself from it.

❑ In this calm state, generate three possible ways you could deal with this situation. Write them down and resolve to take action as soon as you can.

PART II

Unreal Fear—Fear as Foe

CHAPTER 5

Fear in Time

The present has three dimensions… the present of past things, the present of present things and the present of future things.

ST. AUGUSTINE

THE CAUSE OF UNREAL FEAR CAN COME from three different directions—past, present, and future. The stimulus is in the present, but the fear usually comes from imagining the future—what might happen but has not. It can also be about the past—what did happen or what might have happened.

Our mind has a remarkable fluidity with time. Past, present, and future interweave in the present moment—the only place we can act and feel. Intellectually, people put their focus on one as opposed to the others. For example:

❏ Some people believe that the past is the most important. The past makes people who they are now and determines what they do in the future.
❏ Other people believe that the present is the most important. They say that we live in a system of complex cause and effect and we should seek to understand what is happening now in order to know what to do in the future. The present determines what is possible. The past is not important.
❏ Other people say that the future is most important. The past gives us resources to achieve the future we want. Our present desires depend on our future goals.

All of these views have some truth, but none is the whole truth. Perhaps St. Augustine had the best insight in the quote at the beginning of this chapter. The present can change our view of the past and open a new future that we never dreamed was possible. Equally, it can shut off future possibilities.

We are always in the present, and can choose to make the past or the future alive by thinking about it now.

The circles test

There is an interesting exercise developed originally by Thomas Cottle to discover how people approach time. It is known as the "circles test." Try it now. Draw three circles in any way you choose and label them, one representing the past, one representing the present, and one representing the future. Arrange these circles however you want to show the relationship between the three.

Draw your circles here:

Now look at what you have drawn:

Which is the biggest circle?

This can give an indication about which of the three you find the most important.

Where are the circles?

The usual arrangement is for the past, present, and future circles to go left to right, in the same order as we read.

Do they all overlap? Is one circle detached from the others? Which circles have the biggest overlap?

What does this tell you about the way you see the past, present, and future interacting?

Unreal fear in the past

Unreal fear can come from the past. For example, a person may think back to something awful that happened and feel frightened again. An extreme case is post-traumatic stress disorder (PTSD), where a person has had a traumatic experience of war or torture, abuse, or extreme fear, and the memory continues to torment them, sometimes for many years afterward. They cannot deal with the trauma; the body replays it to try to master it. PTSD is beyond the scope of this book, but there are NLP patterns that have been used with good results with victims of torture and abuse (see the reference section on page 241).

Fear of the past usually comes from reviewing an unpleasant experience and feeling anxious about it; for example, giving a very bad speech and wincing every time you remember it. These memories can still intrude in the present and create anxiety. The following NLP pattern can help get rid of this anxiety and stop it spoiling your life in the present. You cannot change the past, you can only learn from it. This pattern helps you do that.

Skill for freedom

Learning from the past

This pattern helps you to learn from the past instead of being afraid of it. It is not suitable for a bad trauma or phobia.

1 Think back to the experience that still makes you anxious. As you do so, stay outside the experience. Make sure that you see yourself in that situation as if on a television or movie screen. You are dissociated from the picture.

2 As you watch this memory unfold from this dissociated point of view, notice what happened at the time, what other people did that contributed to the situation, and how it was impossible for you to control it all.

3 Come out of the memory and start to analyze what happened. How might you avoid similar circumstances in the future?

4 What were you trying to achieve? What did you want to happen?

5 With the benefit of hindsight, how should you have acted in order to get what you wanted?

6 Relive the incident again in your imagination *the way you wanted* it to happen. See yourself doing things differently so you get the result you want. Stay outside the experience; watch yourself acting in the situation on a mental screen.

7 When you are satisfied, imagine stepping into the situation and relive the incident in your imagination, the way you wanted. Be back there,

seeing through your own eyes, acting the way you should have acted and getting the result you wanted. Then blank your mental screen.

8 Do the last step at least five times, reliving the event in the way you would have preferred it to happen, and then blacking out your mental screen at the end of each replay. Do it faster and faster each time.

9 You have just created a new learning experience from the old fear experience.

10 Finally, imagine a similar situation that you might have to face in the future. Rehearse it in exactly the way you want it to happen, associate into the experience, imagine yourself there seeing out of your own eyes and acting in the way you want. Feel it in your muscles. This mental rehearsal will prepare you for the future and ensure that you will not make the same mistake again.

Association and dissociation

The above pattern uses dissociation to separate you from the fear. Dissociation is one of the most important resources against fear.

When you are *dissociated*, you are outside the experience. You have feelings about the experience.

When you are *associated*, you are inside your body looking out through your own eyes. When you are associated, you feel the feelings that go with the experience.

Being associated is like being in the thick of a game; being dissociated is like seeing the same game from the substitutes' bench.

Association is good for enjoying pleasant memories and pleasant experiences. Dissociation is good for keeping a distance from feelings and learning from experience.

When you are in thrall to unreal fear, then you are associated into your mental pictures and this stimulates the fear response. Many of the mental strategies to deal with fear rely on your ability to dissociate from your mental pictures and look on them objectively.

Think of a pleasant memory.

When you think back to it, check what sort of picture you have in your mind.

Are you associated, seeing out through your own eyes?

Or are you dissociated, seeing yourself in the situation?

Whichever one it is, change it and try the other way.

Now change it back to what it was.

Which way do you prefer?

For most people, being associated brings back the feeling more strongly because they are inside their body and so more in touch with their feelings.

Mental rehearsal

The last skill for freedom also used mental rehearsal to help shape the future in the way you want. Mental rehearsal is very important in NLP. We will use this many times in patterns to get rid of unreal fear, because unreal fear is based on imaginings that make us feel bad. We can replace these with imaginings that will make us feel good. When you mentally rehearse what you want, bear the following principles in mind:

❑ *Be clear and specific about what you want.* Imagine it in as much detail as you can.
❑ *Relax.* Relaxation enhances the effects of mental rehearsal.
❑ *Focus on the process as well as the result.* Concentrate on mentally rehearsing everything in detail and the goal will flow naturally from the process.

❏ *Use all your senses*. The more senses you use, the more powerful the rehearsal will be. See the pictures as clearly as you can. Hear the sounds. Feel your body movements, including your sense of balance. Add tastes and smells if they are appropriate in the situation.

❏ *Practice*. Perfect practice makes for perfect results. The more you use mental rehearsal, the more skilled you will become and the better it will work for you. Mentally rehearse the goal at least five times over the course of three days.

Fears of the future

Unreal fears are usually about the future—what *might* happen. Unreal fear, like disappointment, needs adequate planning. As long as you are afraid of the future, it has not happened. This is reassuring. Being afraid of the future does not help; you need to change the way you think about the future to stop feeling afraid now, in the present.

The way to deal with fear of the future is to *act*. The following skill for dealing with future fear applies to many different fears. Use this pattern before any event that is making you anxious. During the actual event (for example if you feel afraid during public performance or flying in an airplane) you need to use the other skills such as relaxation (see page 212).

Skill for freedom

From fear to action

I Acknowledge your anxiety. You feel afraid: do not try to deny it or argue it away.

2 Take some immediate action to calm the anxiety. Relax, slow your

breathing, listen to relaxing music, or otherwise distract yourself. Fear and anxiety make it difficult to think clearly about an issue.

3 Realize that whatever you are afraid of has not happened yet, therefore it exists only as a possibility in your mind. Later you will look back on this fear and laugh.

4 Remember times when you were afraid but everything turned out well. What can you learn from those situations that will help you in this one?

5 Find out what you are imagining that is generating this unreal fear.

What pictures are you seeing?
What do they look like?
What sounds are you hearing?
What are the qualities of the sounds?

6 Once you are aware of exactly how you are creating the anxiety in your imagination, disrupt the pictures and sounds. Blank the pictures. Turn the sounds off, just as you would with a TV program that you do not like.

7 Think about what you want to happen. Make it as clear and specific as possible.

8 Plan some action steps to make that outcome more likely. It is essential to *do* something. Only by taking action can you eliminate unreal fear.

9 Mentally rehearse what you want to happen, not what you fear might happen.

Worry

Unreal fear of the future often appears as worry.

Worry is a choice, not a necessity. It can also be a habit. Worry does have a positive intention—to prepare you for the future and resolve the situation. Many people think it is good to worry, it shows that you "care." However, there are much better ways to show you care for someone than making up bad futures for them. While you manufacture bad possibilities, you remain powerless.

Worry has certain characteristics:

❑ There is a lot of thinking, but no action.
❑ Worry puts you in the spotlight so you feel responsible for what happens. But at the same time, you are powerless; you do not know what to do.
❑ Worry is not directed at a goal, it focuses on avoiding bad situations (which you create because they have not yet happened).
❑ There is no check from the external world. The moment you have information from the external world, you do not worry, you act.

The structure of worry

Once you understand the structure of worry, it will lose some of its power because now you know what is happening and you can stop it and move in a more constructive direction.

Worry always has the same structure. First, there is a trigger event that usually leads to some internal dialogue: "What if X were to happen?"

This internal dialogue usually leads to constructed pictures of the bad event described by the internal dialogue. These pictures are usually bright, colorful, and draw you into their story. You associate into them and once you are associated, you feel anxious, they are really happening now in your imagination.

Overleaf is the antidote to worry.

Skill for freedom

From worry to action

1 Become aware of your internal dialogue. Instead of asking "What if X were to happen?" ask instead "What will I do if X happens?"

This has three effects:

- ❑ It puts the events into the future.
- ❑ You dissociate from them.
- ❑ It changes your attention from the events to your actions. You can now plan what to do.

Sometimes this is enough for you to recognize the ridiculous scenarios and to stop spinning in the worry loop. However, if the scenarios are serious and likely and you need to plan, go on to the next step.

2 Make some dissociated pictures of what you can do to help the situation—see yourself in the pictures doing what is necessary to deal with it. Choose one possibility that makes you feel good.

3 Mentally rehearse that plan—imagine yourself taking that action. Associate into this plan, feel yourself there doing what you have decided. After that, you can stop worrying because you have decided to do something to help yourself.

If you cannot find any plan with which you are completely satisfied, then pick the best you have. Sometimes it is enough to get more information about the situation.

CHAPTER 6

Common Fears that Hold Us Hostage

I have had thousands of problems in my life—most of which have never happened.
MARK TWAIN

UNREAL FEARS ARE THOSE WE HAVE LEARNED to create in response to anchors. Once we understand how we *learn* them, we can use the same mechanism to *unlearn* them with NLP.

NLP proposes that we create unreal fears through our mental strategies. A strategy is a series of thoughts: pictures, sounds, or feelings with an outcome. The key to getting rid of unreal fear is to change your strategy.

Here is the basic strategy that creates unreal fear:

❑ React to an anchor from the outside world.
❑ Make bright, colorful, moving pictures of events that you do not want to happen.
❑ Associate with them so you feel you are inside the mental picture you are creating.
❑ Try to fight the feeling, when you should be dealing with the process that generated the feeling.

The antidote is to discover what frightening scenario you are creating in your imagination and then dissociate from it. Substitute an imagining of what you want to happen instead.

In this chapter we will use this NLP technique on a number of common fears.

Fear of flying

Many people are afraid of flying, especially after the tragedy of September 11th. When you are on an aircraft you have no control, and unless you are in business or first class you are squashed into a small space, surrounded by strangers in a claustrophobic atmosphere.

People are afraid of flying for two reasons: the *consequences* of something going wrong and the *risk* of something going wrong. Although the risk of something going wrong is very small, the consequences would be fatal.

Flying is uncomfortable, but very safe. Most people who are afraid of flying really fear turbulence. Once the plane starts to jump and vibrate it seems like it is falling to pieces, but the plane needs to be flexible. A tree bends in the wind and stays upright. Buildings in earthquake areas are built so they can vibrate with any earth tremor rather than staying rigid and trying to resist the tremors. Flexibility means survival. When the plane shakes in turbulence this is a good sign: it is exactly what should happen. Turbulence never hurt any aircraft, although it can be alarming.

Some people are afraid of turbulence, yet are willing to pay for a rollercoaster or fairground ride that will pitch them about far more. I do not mind the feeling of turbulence, but I must admit that my heart skips a beat if the engine noise changes, I am more sensitive to the sound of the engines than to the smoothness of the ride.

Some people have problems about being high and do not like to look down. If so, you can play with perspective. When you look out of a window and see small objects, there are two possibilities. One is that they are large objects a long way away. The other alternative is that they are small objects close up. Looking out of the window and imagining that everything you see is small and close can take away the fear of being up high.

Many people fear aircraft because they feel they have no control over what happens. Yet they will happily take a ride in a car driven by a friend, where they have no control and have a statistically much higher chance of being involved in an accident. They take this for granted because it is familiar.

Fear of flying can be dealt with by applying the fear to action skill. When you feel anxious about an impending flight, do the following.

Skill for freedom

Fear of flying pattern

---

1 Acknowledge your fear. Relax and breathe freely. You are still on the ground.

2 What are you imagining? Nearly everyone I have helped with this fear had a very unpleasant mental picture at the back of their mind. It was usually a small, dark picture of a cramped aircraft seat. They were trapped there and the plane was pitching wildly in extreme turbulence, before plunging straight down to the ground. They were associated into the picture, so they got the bad feelings of being in a turbulent aircraft. They had no control. They were afraid of the picture, not of what was happening. They hardly noticed the flight because the internal picture was so alarming.

3 Dissociate from the picture. See yourself in the aircraft from the outside.

4 Experiment with the qualities of the picture:
   a   Make the picture larger.
   b   Make it fuzzy.
   c   Make it black and white.
   d   Make it smooth and still.

   Some or all of these changes will make the picture have less impact.

5 Listen to what you are telling yourself. What are you saying to yourself about the flight?

Experiment with the voice tone. Make it faster or slower. Make it squeaky or musical. Laugh at it.

6 What is the positive intention of the voice? It is probably to keep you safe. Change the words so that they express a useful positive intention. For example, you could change "It will be an awful flight" to "I will enjoy a smooth flight."

7 Set your goal. You want a smooth, trouble-free flight.

8 Mentally rehearse. Imagine being on a calm, safe flight. Be associated in the picture. Close your eyes and imagine you are in a comfortable. spacious seat. Be there, seeing through your own eyes and enjoying the good feelings. See yourself there smiling and enjoying the flight. When you are happy with that picture, associate into it. Feel comfort able. You are creating the reality you want in your mind and enjoying it. Before you created a frightening picture. Now you are creating a pleasant, safe scenario. Which would you rather live in?

If you feel afraid when you are in the air:

❏ Become aware of your feelings, and be curious about what you are feeling.
❏ Relax your body (see page 212).
❏ Use a safety anchor (page 220).

Fear of authority

Many people are frightened of authority figures—a fear that often starts in childhood, where authority is power and has both the ability and the permission to hurt. They feel like a child again and are powerless to stand up for themselves. It is strange that the word "authority" comes from the Latin *auctor*, the same root as "author"— someone who creates. In a twist worthy of George Orwell, authority figures usually try to maintain the status quo rather than create anything new.

Authority is not something a person has by themselves, it is given. We give authority figures their power. Some professions are essential and are there to serve us, like the police or public servants. Other people are placed above us in business and this authority should be grounded in their knowledge and skill, otherwise they do not deserve respect. Authority usually derives from a role: a manager, a guard, a police officer, a teacher. They are there for a reason and that reason is usually to help you.

Sometimes the person who fills that role does so unworthily. They use it to put other people down so they can feel good about themselves. We have all met people like that. Some of them are in a position to hurt us. Separate the role of the authority figure from the person who occupies it, which will stop any generalization of bad experiences from one figure to another. Just because one manager is bad does not mean they all are. The next one you meet might be fine. To look at authority in a new perspective, we will use the NLP idea of perceptual positions.

Perceptual positions

To understand a situation completely you need to take different perspectives, just like looking at an object from different angles to see its breadth, height, and depth. One angle doesn't give all the information you need. NLP has evolved three perspectives or ways of looking at a situation, known as first, second, and third perceptual positions.

First position is your own reality, your own view of any situation. It is what you feel, think, and believe in that moment.

Second position is making a creative leap to understand the world from another person's perspective, to think the way *they* think. Second position is the basis of empathy and rapport. It allows you to appreciate another person's feelings about the situation. It is essential in any type of negotiation to understand the other person's position from their point of view.

Third position is to step outside your view, to a detached perspective. You are not taking either your position or another person's position. You see the relationships between the two viewpoints and assess them objectively.

All the three positions are useful; most people have a habitual one.

One way you can use second position to help with fear is to imagine you are someone else. Borrow an identity (for example a superhero) and then imagine how they would feel. It is a little game that can help.

We feel inferior because of how we perceive authority. The next skill using perceptual positions will change the way you see authority.

Skill for freedom

Fear of authority pattern

I Think about a situation with an authority figure where you feel afraid.

What do you see?
What feelings do you have?
Are there any internal voices? If so, what are they saying?
What are you mostly aware of?

This gives you a clear awareness of what the situation is like, so you can compare how you feel after this process.

2 Imagine yourself in second position.

Imagine you are the authority figure.
What is that like? How does it feel?
Come back and be yourself again.

This does not mean that you like or agree with the authority figure. It is only a means of understanding.

3 Go to third position.

See yourself and the authority figure together.
Make sure that you are equidistant from the "you" you see and the
authority figure.
In your mental picture, make sure that you are:

❑ Observing from eye level (not from above or below).
❑ Hearing your own voice and the authority's voice coming from
   where you see them (not as a disembodied voice).
❑ Speaking from your throat area.
❑ Hearing your real voice (not a childish voice).
❑ Hearing their real voice (not a parental voice).
❑ Feeling resourceful. Put all the unresourceful feelings with the
   "you" that you see in the picture.
❑ Feeling fully balanced, standing up.

How does this change your experience?
Be fully aware of what it is like to see the situation from the outside
and not be drawn into it.

4 Go back to first position.

Imagine yourself in the problem situation again with the authority
figure. Make sure that you are:

❑ Seeing the other person exactly out in front of you.
❑ Hearing the other person's real voice coming from their mouth.
❑ Feeling your own real voice coming from your throat area.

In this position, say: "I am here." Feel the force of the statement.
What changes when you do this?
How do you feel now?

This skill works because the fear comes not from the authority itself,
but from how you are thinking about it. By changing how you think
about it, the fear diminishes and it is represented in a more realistic

way. People in authority are just people, they go home and eat and sleep like anyone else.

Fear of success

Sometimes success brings unexpected problems, or we set out to achieve a goal and then become apprehensive as we approach it.

The first steps toward a goal are the easiest and get the most obvious results. As time goes on and you need to make more effort and face the law of decreasing returns, the same effort gets you less. The closer you get, the more effort you need to advance and improve. When success really is within our grasp, we start to see all the other consequences that up to now we have not considered. We fear these consequences, rather than the goal. That is when we might "choke."

For example, a man wants to become a millionaire, he works hard, and amasses a lot of money. As he nears that magic million, he suddenly notices how many of his friends seem to be more interested in his money than himself. He notices how little he knows his family, and how the money has not brought him the happiness he thought it would. He doubts his goal. Then he may sabotage his success, because it brings too many other undesirable consequences.

NLP uses *ecology* to describe the further consequences of a goal. Fear of success is often a fear of these unforeseen consequences. To avoid this situation, you need a continuous ecology check.

Skill for freedom

Ecology check

Establish your goal—what you want and do not have.

Imagine yourself having achieved the goal. Go fully into that situation.

Where will you be?

Who will you be with?
What will be happening?
How will you feel?

When you can imagine yourself fully inside that goal, completely associated, come out and you will be in a good position to answer these questions:

❏ What are the traps and pitfalls on that journey that you want to avoid?
Think about the things that you want to avoid *en route* to the goal. Goals are not achieved instantaneously, you have to take a journey.

❏ Now think about those things that you will have to give up, those things that you have and want to keep. Are you prepared to do that? What is important about your present circumstances that you want to keep?

❏ What will be the consequences for the people you know who are close to you? Put yourself in their position. (Take second position with them.)
What will they think when you achieve your goal?
What can you do to make sure that they are not badly affected?

❏ What else will happen or could happen because of achieving your goal?

❏ What other goals will you have to put on hold or give up if you achieve this one? Goals need time and money and neither of these resources is unlimited. There is an opportunity cost to every goal— those goals you might have got but now will not because you are using your resources on this one.

These questions will help you explore the goal and make sure that success is something to be welcomed rather than feared.

Fear of dentists and doctors

Many people are afraid of going to the doctor or the dentist. They do not run away from such people at a party (instead they may talk to them at great length), but they are afraid of what might happen when they visit them in a professional capacity.

Because people often go to the doctor for reassurance that they are not ill, they may *not* go when something really is wrong with them and they need treatment. The doctor or dentist is a bringer of bad news. This is a fear of an imaginary future and can be dealt with by the worry pattern (page 72) or the fear to action pattern (page 69). Sometimes people avoid visiting the dentist or doctor at all costs; they would rather be ill or in pain. Relaxation exercises (see page 212) are useful for becoming calm before or during the appointment.

Fear of heights

Fear of heights is common and is probably left over from the instinctual fear we have of falling as infants. However, fear of heights is not inevitable, else there would be no mountaineers and no pilots. Being uncomfortable with heights is not a problem unless it stops you flying, living above the ground floor, or appreciating a wonderful view. As long as your vantage point is safe (such as a balcony) then there is no real danger.

Deal with fear of heights by using some of these skills:

❑ Use a relaxation pattern (page 212).
❑ Use a safety anchor and relax your body to calm the fear (page 220).
❑ Look and see what mental pictures you are making (usually of you falling or being whirled away into space and then falling).
❑ Dissociate from the pictures.
❑ Picture yourself enjoying the view and then enjoy it.

Fear of elevators

Elevators manage to combine two fears: fear of enclosed spaces and fear of heights. When I visited one of the tallest buildings in the world, I felt a little uncomfortable. We were in Hong Kong and one building on Hong Kong Island with the unexciting name of Two International Finance Centre has over 80 floors. Visitors can take a lift only to the 55th floor, but this was quite enough for me. The lift was very good: it ascended for less than a minute at a constant acceleration, so I did not feel I was moving. The view over the bay was magnificent.

Fear of elevators and heights are dealt with in exactly the same way as other fears:

❏ Relax (page 212).
❏ Use a safety anchor and relax your body to calm the fear (page 220).
❏ Look and see what mental pictures you are making (usually pictures of the lift plummeting out of control or the lights going out and being stuck between floors).
❏ Dissociate from the pictures.
❏ Picture yourself enjoying the ride and concentrate on where you are going to arrive rather than on the elevator ride itself.

Fear of death

As George Bernard Shaw said: "Life does not cease to be fun when people die any more than it ceases to be serious when people laugh."

Many people fear death; it is the ultimate loss—loss of life. This fear keeps us safe: it stops us taking stupid risks. Fear of death only becomes a problem if it preoccupies your thoughts or makes you anxious. Fear of death is similar to other worries about the future, but here we know that eventually it will come true. We just do not know when.

One reason death has the power to frighten is that we deny it most of the time. Nearly everywhere in the world it is illegal to die of old age, the World Health Organization does not allow it. Everyone must die of a specific cause; "old age" is inadmissible on a death certificate, even though doctors know it is an adequate statement because our bodies are not exempt from the law of entropy.

Only one third of the adult population of England has made a will. It is not that the others have nothing to leave, but a will is an uncomfortable reminder of your own mortality, as if to think about death might somehow invite it. Yet making a will is common sense: it allows your affairs to be settled more quickly and in a less distressing way for friends and family. Denying death gives it the power to frighten us and means we may be unprepared.

Death is a fact of life. Everyone will die, and this is what gives life its meaning. There is a proverb: "Dream as if you will never die, but live and act to achieve your goals as if you will die tomorrow." Our dreams should be wide and unlimited; they define the scope of our life. Then we should take action and put those dreams into reality. Without a sense of urgency, the dreams remain just dreams. Death makes us take action. Actors cannot give a good performance if the curtain never falls, athletes cannot pace themselves without a finishing tape, and musicians cannot shape their performance without a final chord. Death is not something to be afraid of; death need not be painful.

One thing we can do to reduce the fear of death is to make it an adviser to tell us what is the most important thing for us to do in the present. Here is one skill you can use that will make the idea of death enrich your life right now.

The next skill is best done in a quiet place in a relaxed frame of mind.

Skill for freedom

Death as an adviser

Imagine yourself in the far future, looking back on your life now.

What do you want to have accomplished by this point?
What important goals do you have that remain dreams?
What would it feel like to have accomplished these things?
Is there anything you need to do now to prepare for the time when you die and are no longer here to take care of people and do the things you enjoy doing?
What advice can you give to the you now, from this place in the far future?
How important are the worries of your present self from this distant point of view?
What is the most important thing that you need to do now?

Come back to the present moment, and reflect a little on what you have learned.

In the words of a Tibetan proverb: "It is better to have lived one day as a tiger, than one thousand years as a sheep."

Think of this next time you feel unreal fear.

CHAPTER 7

Unquiet Times and Turbulent Minds

Good people do not need laws to tell them to act responsibly, while bad people will find a way around the laws.

PLATO

WE ALL HAVE INDIVIDUAL FEARS that come from our personal history. Our culture also adds to our burden of fear. "Now is the age of Anxiety," wrote W. H. Auden nearly 50 years ago in his poem "A Baroque Eclogue." An eclogue is a short pastoral poem, although Auden's work was far from pastoral. It was about the human quest to find some identity in an increasingly industrialized world. It won the Pulitzer Prize for poetry in 1948.

The postindustrial society is here; we live in unquiet times. There is an undercurrent of vague fear, like shapes in the mist, hard to pin down, but we may feel it when we turn on our television, listen to the radio, or surf the internet. This miasma of fear does not belong to anyone; it is our collective heritage. This chapter is about these shapes in the mist. Once we can see them clearly, we can deal with them more easily. We can unlearn the cultural thinking that gives these fears their power.

Dangerous places

First, the clear and present dangers. Some countries are inherently more dangerous than others. There are countries wracked by war, where violent death is commonplace. There are many excellent books by war correspondents about what it is like to live in such places, full of authentic danger. *Forbes* magazine maintains an updated list of the world's most dangerous destinations. At the end of 2004 it listed Afghanistan, Haiti, Iraq, Liberia, Pakistan, Somalia, Yemen, and Zimbabwe as the most dangerous destinations (not necessarily in that order).

In every country, there are places that are more dangerous than others. And in every big city, there are areas where only the very confident, the very knowing, or the very foolish will tread at night. Geneva-based Mercer Human Resource Consulting keeps another list of 200 of the most dangerous cities in the world, based on factors such as crime levels, law enforcement, and internal stability. Luxembourg is the safest city according to this study. The Central African City of Bangui is considered the least safe. Bad news for the Central African Tourist Board.

Even normally safe cities can experience disaster. For example, Madrid is a very pleasant and safe city, yet it experienced a terrible bomb outrage in 2004. Tokyo is also a safe city, but a few years ago a terrorist group released poison gas in the metro.

When people feel comfortable and safe, disasters like these are not just terrible—they are surprising. They make people question their basic assumptions about their personal safety and how the world is. We are not as safe as we thought. What else might happen? Such disasters usually lead to stricter laws in the hope of controlling the future. Politicians pledge that this kind of event must never happen again.

Personal safety

Feeling safe is a basic human need. Whatever the dangers of the place where we live, we adjust and take sensible precautions—sensible for that area. For example, I live in São Paulo, Brazil. There are no terrorist threats, but there is more crime here than in most European cities. There are many more poor and homeless people. An ordinary wage earner is privileged. Most people live either in closed condominiums with patrolling security guards, or in high apartment blocks, again with guards and security on the gates. Houses have grilles on the windows and high walls, often with electric fences.

At night, cars approach red lights slowly, trying to keep moving. If the light is still red when they reach it, they go through anyway if they can in safety. This is sensible in a city where you are at risk of being robbed in a stationary car late at night. Even during the day, a red light is often taken as a suggestion rather than a legal requirement. In contrast, there is little danger of being robbed in your car in most parts of London, so people respect the lights. Brazilians think this is crazy. Londoners think Brazilians are crazy, but when you put the behaviors in their cultural context, both are sensible.

It reminds me of the joke about a man hailing a taxi late at night in Brazil. He gets in and starts to chat with the cab driver. The driver approaches a red light and goes straight through it. The man says nothing (probably being a diplomatic Englishman, not wanting to make trouble), but when it happens a second time, he cannot stop himself.

"Excuse me, but shouldn't you stop at red lights?" he asks.

"Oh, don't worry, my cousin taught me to drive. He always goes through red lights and he has never had an accident."

The passenger stays quiet until the cab driver goes fast down a one-way street in the wrong direction.

"Excuse me, wasn't that a one-way street?"

"Sure," says the cab driver, "But my cousin showed me how to do this. If you go really fast, you can get through before you meet any traffic coming the other way."

"I see," says the passenger, hanging on to the seat belt and wondering about his chances of getting another cab at that time of night.

Then suddenly the cab driver starts to drive with exaggerated care. He stops at every light, red or green. He obeys all the traffic signs.

"Thank you," says the passenger. "I feel much safer."

"So do I," says the cab driver. "My cousin lives around this area."

Many expensive cars in South America are bullet proofed as a matter of course, because the rich are in danger of being kidnapped. Bullet proofing is as common as a 10,000-mile service. In England, people would think you were crazy if you bullet-proofed your BMW. In South America, people go even further. They make the car impregnable and fit a sound system so you can talk to someone outside without having to leave the car or wind down the windows. These are sensible precautions for rich people in large South American and Central American cities. You can be robbed in any city, though. You have to take sensible precautions based on where you are.

Laws and safety

Our safety always depends on the goodwill of other people. Anyone with a grudge or a crazy idea can cause a lot of damage with existing technology, and we have entered an age where they are willing to carry out their threats. Unquiet people make for unquiet times. People with crazy ideas do not play by the rules and the results are unpredictable and frightening.

We try to make the world completely safe by removing the dangers one by one. When we recognize a new danger we pass legislation to try to ensure it does not happen again. When someone goes berserk with a gun, we pass new gun laws. When a dog savages a child, there are curbs on dangerous dogs. These are good responses, but passing a law does not remove the danger. A law does not stop people. It may deter them, unless they have nothing to lose. It does ensure that the people who break it are punished (but only if they are caught). The quote from Plato at the beginning of the chapter shows the paradox. Laws mostly deter law-abiding people.

In Europe and the United States, familiar freedoms are vanishing because some people have abused them. The UK is going to introduce identity cards, voluntary for now, but they will surely be compulsory in ten years. Governments like to control their citizens, and freedoms once gone are hard to reclaim. There will always be a social debate about whether everyone should suffer because of the actions of a few madmen. This debate was especially strong after the September 11th terrorist attack.

Danger and the media

Why is living perceived to be more dangerous now? One reason is that the media constantly present danger and the threat of danger. Contented people living safely in their houses are not news and do not get reported. Violence, unrest, and the threat of disaster are news. They get reported (and often exaggerated). Many people feel a bizarre sense of pleasure at the possibility of disaster. It may be bad, but then at least they can say "I told you so." It is perversely satisfying to be able to top your friend's horror story with one a little worse. The "news" has to be new. And it has to pack more punch than the last news, otherwise it is boring repetition. The first shooting is news. A second is not. Yet every shooting is real and painful and tragic for the real people that are involved in it. The media sentimentalize the news, they cannot help it. News is always about other people.

The media add to our burden of fear. A personal tragedy hurts. A thousand personal tragedies are too much to take in and are passed on to a government agency to take care of. Terrorists are taking more drastic action to get attention.

Social anxiety and stress

The results of this are twofold. First, we become less sensitive to pain and tragedy. We are used to it. We build up psychic scar tissue to defend against it. Secondly, films, television, and stories have to push the boundaries in order to get a reaction. We laugh at the horror tales that once stirred our parents. Films like *Se7en* and *Saw* set the standards now. At the deepest level, we still have the fear reaction that evolution has given us and it is constantly being stimulated.

Biological evolution cannot keep pace with social evolution: we still have the fear response of our cave-dwelling ancestors, who experienced everything first hand and not through a television screen. So we suffer constant low-grade anxiety and stress. Like a chronic illness, it saps our strength, but doesn't show up on a test.

Stress is a metaphor. It comes from the field of physics and describes the force applied and also the resulting damage. We are stressed when we are pushed repeatedly beyond our natural ability to cope.

We described the physiological reaction to fear in Chapter 1 (see page 17). The fear reaction is meant to be a short-term response to immediate danger. When this reaction becomes chronic, we suffer stress; this state of arousal becomes normal. Some people become addicted to stress, they like the biochemical cocktail, it makes them feel more alive. They need a greater and greater level to attain the same high. But stress increases our blood pressure, raises the heart rate, disturbs digestion, and impairs our thinking. The body needs time to recover and to replenish the supply of hormones and neurotransmitters that are used in the fear response

Dealing with str

How can we deal with this low-grade anxiety and stress? First, know the difference between your area of concern and area of influence.

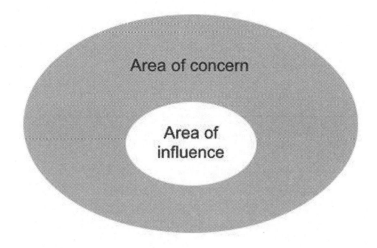

In the area of concern are those things we care about. In the area of influence are those things we can do something about. The area of influence is much smaller than the area of concern. Trying to influence the whole area of concern leads to a lot of stress and an increased risk of heart disease and gastric illness. The other extreme is feeling helpless and failing to do anything in situations that are within our area of influence.

When you feel stress, you may either be worrying about something you cannot influence, or feeling helpless in the face of too many demands.

Perhaps this was best summed up by the theologian Reinhold Niebuhr, when he wrote: "God give us the grace to accept with serenity the things that cannot be changed, courage to change the things that should be changed, and the wisdom to distinguish one from the other."

Skill for freedom

Dealing with stress

1 Acknowledge the stress you feel. You may feel you "should not" be stressed, but observe what is there without judging yourself.

2 Focus on what stimulus you think is making you feel like this. Go through all the possibilities. Pay attention to what you have seen on the television and in the news recently.

3 What can you do about it?

Is it in your area of influence? If not, let it go and move on.

If it is in your area of influence, what can you do? There may be very little: giving a donation or taking part in an election may be the only thing. But at least you have done something. Then let it go.

CHAPTER 8

Social Fears

Things do not change—we change.
HENRY DAVID THOREAU

WE FACE MANY UNSPECIFIC FEARS IN DAY-TO-DAY LIVING, and they can be stressful. We will deal with some of the common ones in this chapter.

Change

Change need not be threatening, but the high rate of change in modern society is hard to deal with. We have to run to stay in the same place. We walk toward the future with no light to guide us; this means uncertainty and uncertainty means fear.

There is a joke about the difference between US and Japanese business. American business adopts a "Ready?... Fire!" approach. Japanese business instead uses "Ready?... Aim... Aim... Aim... Aim... Fire!" Now all businesses are trying a third approach: "Ready or not... Fire!" There is no time to aim.

Our biology does not equip us to deal with this fast and unprecedented rate of change. Our minds leap ahead, but our bodies are still in most ways the same as when they evolved some hundreds of thousands of years ago. We do not have the biology to deal with jet lag, a diet of fast food, a polluted atmosphere, or cramped living spaces.

Computer technology enables many things that were unbelievable 20 years ago. We can do more, and faster. It is a short step to say that we *should* do more, and do it faster.

I remember my first personal computer, which I bought in 1984. It boasted a huge (for that time) 32MB hard drive, which now would not even store this book in my wordprocessing program. Programs came on cassette audiotapes and could take up to 20 minutes to load. If there was something wrong with the audiotape (and we know how temperamental they can be), the program would stop and I had start again from the beginning. I tolerated this because I enjoyed using the computer and that was the way it worked. Gradually everything got faster. Floppy disks were a big improvement on cassette tapes. Then came CDs, then detachable hard drives. Each computer I bought was more powerful and faster than the last. Now, I sit here and load programs in a few seconds. And I am used to that. So if it takes five seconds rather than two seconds to load, I notice. If it takes ten seconds then I start drumming my fingers in frustration. We become accustomed to the new fast pace—not the absolute speed, but our *perception* of the speed. However quickly computers work, we soon become used to it and become frustrated when it doesn't happen.

The same principles apply to the internet. When the World Wide Web first appeared, most people using it had a modem. Now a modem seems ridiculously slow compared with broadband. Nevertheless, there is no convincing research to show that faster computers let us work faster. We can do more, but there is more to do. Computers *create* work. They provide many more possible distractions (web surfing, chat, games), and many businesses are less productive than they were. We will look at change in detail and how to deal with it in Chapter 10.

Time pressure

It seems the faster we do things, the more we find ourselves under time pressure. Everything should have been done yesterday or sooner. Time has become a precious, scarce resource, and there are huge numbers of time management courses and books. These fail unless they take into account two things: people's beliefs and the way they view time. Many people use time management techniques successfully to free up time in their day, but then they feel guilty and fill that "free" time with something else. Then they feel under pressure again. At the end of the time management course they are still doing too much.

We all face deadlines in our life and work. As they inexorably approach, some people are paralyzed by indecision, and the deadline is disturbing, not motivating.

Others need a deadline to motivate them and they wait until the last minute before finishing. This strategy puts a lot of stress on those who want to do the work early. A partnership where one person wants to finish the work in plenty of time and the other does it at the last minute is heading for disaster unless both parties understand each other and manage the situation. They will not want to collaborate again except under duress.

The reason people think differently about deadlines is because they have different attitudes to time. NLP proposes that we experience time as distance—as a timeline. We use distance to measure time: a day is measured as 24 times the circumference of a clock. We talk of the distant past, the far future, being close to things. How you think about time is the most important element in how you deal with deadlines.

Skill for freedom

Dealing with deadlines

What do you think of deadlines?

Think of a deadline that you have to meet, or imagine that you have a deadline.

What does it look like to you?
How big does it seem?
Where in space does this deadline seem to be compared to now?
How far away does it seem to be?
How does that distance correspond to time?

(For example, if your deadline is a week away, how far away does it seem when you picture it in your mind? What distance corresponds with a week?)

Mentally move the deadline further away. How do you feel about that? Are you more or less motivated?

Now imagine moving it closer. Move it very close. How do you feel about that? Is it more motivating? Is it more stressful or disturbing?

Move it to a distance that feels comfortable. You have not changed the date in reality, but you may feel less stressed about it because you are thinking about it differently.

The people who are most stressed by deadlines are those who imagine them very close on their timeline—regardless of how far away they are in reality. The deadline may be weeks off, but in their mind it looms large and close. One good way to stop the stress of a deadline is to make sure you picture it in a pleasant color at a comfortable distance.

Experiment with how you imagine the deadline until you find the distance that works best for you. Of course, you still have to do the work, but the way you think about the deadline will be making you feel good instead of stressed.

Appearances

Here is a fear that never goes away—the fear of not looking good. There is tremendous pressure on everyone to appear at their best all the time, and this pressure is worse for women than for men. The stereotypes for beauty are more severe and less forgiving for women and women are judged more on their appearance. Looking back in history, the most influential women were often thought to be so because of their beauty. Men are judged by their power and influence, women by their beauty.

Fashion and the media set standards and they are mostly unrealistic. In the UK and Europe, top fashion models and icons of beauty are often thin to the point that they look anorexic. Photographs are altered so that the models look even more perfect. No one looks like this in reality, but the images have power. In a recent survey in the UK, a large percentage of teenagers said that they were dissatisfied with their bodies and were actively considering plastic surgery.

In Brazil there is also a strong focus on outward appearance, although Brazilians do not consider a very thin body attractive. For them an attractive body has muscles. In the UK the gyms are full of people who need to be there: they are overweight and unfit. In Brazil the gyms are full of people who look like they shouldn't be there by British standards—they are muscular, fit, and look great. But they feel that the pressure is there to keep looking this way, especially women.

In many different cultures appearance has become mistaken for identity: people think if their appearance is not good, people will not like them as individuals. If they change appearance, they change identity. If a politician wants power, they get a makeover. This leads to a self-fulfilling prophecy where physically attractive people generally get more opportunities to make money and have a good career. It is a culture for chameleons, not people.

A friend gave me an example. She is normally smartly dressed and buys clothes every week. One day she came to work well dressed and with a gold necklace. Her boss, who generally likes her and values her work, told her that the necklace was not appropriate. She felt uncomfortable and that she had lost some credibility at work.

The underlying fear is of people not liking us. It can mean loss of a job, of money, of a relationship, or of self-esteem. Pressure comes from everywhere—the media, our friends, our boss, our colleagues. We feel afraid if we cannot meet the standards they set.

Look your best, be healthy, make the most of yourself, but do not be anxious about unrealistic comparisons and judgments. Your best is good enough. You are not defined by how you look.

It is possible to use NLP to deal with some of the unreal fear that judging by appearances can generate.

Skill for freedom

Not judging by appearances

Use this skill when you feel afraid that you do not look good enough.

1 Listen to your internal dialogue. Are you saying that you are not going to be good enough?

By what standards are you judging yourself? Where did you get these standards:

❑ Your parents?
❑ The media?

Are these standards realistic?

Are these standards your standards?

Who exactly is judging you?

Are you sure they care as much as you think?

How will you know when you look good enough?

If you cannot answer this last question, then you can never be sure if you will be good enough.

Do the best you can now.

2 Remember, this is just one moment in your life. It does not mean that everybody will think you look bad, and this will be the case far into the future.

3 Listen to your internal dialogue. Are you telling yourself that you should look better? Listen for words like "should," "have to," and "must." These are pressure words.

What would happen if you did not conform?
What forces you? Is it really necessary?
Just suppose you didn't have to—what would that be like?

If there are good, objective reasons for putting on a good appearance to a certain well-defined standard, then do so. Otherwise think twice.

4. Check the mental picture you have of yourself. Is it good? Make it brighter and more colorful. You may be paying more attention to your internal picture than you are to the real you.

5 Remember that your appearance is not you: it is something you choose. How you appear does not define your identity. How would you like to define who you really are?

Fear of the future

The future is not what it used to be. It is more uncertain; we wonder what sort of life we are bequeathing to our grandchildren.

There are many more ways for things to go wrong than for them to go right, and many future scenarios are frightening. Pessimists will remind you that many countries are at war, and that these wars are more bitterly fought than ever. Terrorists kill civilians in the name of their cause. The "war against terror" that the US is fighting has the potential to start many more full scale wars like those in Afghanistan and Iraq. Large companies are involved in corporate scandals. Many people no longer trust big business to act ethically or even sensibly. On the environmental front, there is some evidence of shifts in the global climate; chemical waste and pollution seep into the environment, with many chemicals taking thousands of years to degrade. Are we poisoning our world? In some countries, social services that we take for granted are at breaking point. In many Latin American cities, electricity and water are rationed to certain times of day. People with money are retreating to closed condominium complexes patrolled by security guards and surrounded by electric fences. Furthermore, advances in genetic manipulation have opened up questions about eugenics, designer babies, and a host of ethical problems that we have never confronted before. Have we lost control? Are we on a slippery slope and it is too late to put the brakes on even if we try?

With the focus on bad news, it can seem like the world is falling apart—nothing is safe. But generalizing in this pessimistic way only makes us feel worse. There is good medical evidence that pessimistic thinking damages your health. This statistical link is more robust than that between smoking and lung cancer.

Optimists counter by saying that many well-intentioned and intelligent people are working for peace, and that we can put technology to work to solve these problems. We will discover new ways to produce fresh water and to counter pollution. The age of mass space travel is only a generation away, and this will spawn new technologies that will help solve problems here on Earth. Genetic advances will let people live healthier, happier lives and genetic defects will be eradicated.

It has been said (attributed to James Cabell) that the optimist proclaims we live in the best of all possible worlds, and the pessimist fears that this is true.

Both the optimistic and the pessimistic views are predictions, not reality. We make one or the other real by the decisions we take now. We have to think globally and act locally. People acting in their best interests without looking at the bigger picture usually *cause* difficulties. We can all work for a better future for all by doing our best to give a better life to those we love. We cannot solve such large-scale problems on our own, but we are not powerless—we all have a circle of influence, however small. We can work with other people; one candle can light a thousand others. Those who caused the greatest revolutions in philosophy, science, technology, and ethics were not politicians; most had no secular power at all.

Remember the well-known metaphor from chaos theory: a butterfly flapping its wings in Rio de Janeiro can cause a tornado in Texas. The weather system is so complex that a very small disturbance can be magnified by air currents to create a huge disturbance thousands of miles away. In the same way, a small act of kindness or an intelligent decision can have effects on many other people far beyond the immediate environment. Fear of the future can be a healthy motivation to make good decisions. The future is made now.

Information

The information you can obtain is not the information you want... The information you want is not the information you need... The information you need is not the information you can obtain...

Good information is crucial to feeling safe. We used to have a problem getting information and it was precious. Now we have the opposite problem: information is so plentiful that sometimes it is worth nothing. For example, I wanted to research "fear of flying" on the internet, so I typed the words into the Google search engine. Back came 3,250,000 hits in 0.14 seconds. Information overload. Now what? How can I find exactly what I am looking for? The information I want is hidden somewhere in those hits, but where? I don't have a lifetime to sift through them all. Three and a quarter million pieces of information is as good (or as bad) as none. Google ranks these results, but the way it ranks them may not correspond with my exact interest.

Scientific knowledge has increased exponentially in the last century, so the answer to your question is probably out there; the problem is to find it. It is harder to get good information, and there is always the sneaking feeling that you may be missing something important.

There is a game called Googlewhacking. Its object is to put two words into the Google search engine that will bring up only one web page as the answer. This is not easy. If the words are too unconnected and esoteric, no pages are returned. If the words are too general, there will be more than one. One of the first Googlewhacks was "ambidextrous scallywags." Now there are over 100 pages returned for that combination of words. Googlewhacking is a joke, but behind the humor it is clear that the only way to get through the information glut is to hone the art of asking good questions.

We need information that is as precise and relevant as possible. The most important skill is to ask exactly the right question. The quality of the information you get depends on the quality of the question you ask—this is the GIGO principle (garbage in garbage out).

The internet also offers us ezines and newsgroups on every conceivable subject. Many are interesting, but we cannot read them all. It is an Aladdin's cave of goodies seducing us further and further in; and the further in we go, the more there is available. The internet is open 24/7. It does not sleep, but we have to.

Too much email is also information overload. Email is an example of the "tragedy of the commons." What started as useful, quick, and easy can be useless, slow, and difficult because so many people use it. Spam is one problem. You didn't ask for it, you don't want it, yet it keeps coming in floods—drugs, porn, personalized messages telling you have won the lottery, and solicitations from unknown Nigerian businesspeople to open up your bank account to them. The real, important email gets lost in the slush pile. No wonder looking at their inbox on Monday morning causes anxiety for many people. So much to do, and so little guidance on what is important.

The best way to deal with information overload is to be absolutely clear about your goal. Then ask the precise question that gets you the information you need for your goal and no more.

It is important to limit the information you take in. Too much information just leads to confusion and a turbulent mind.

Skill for freedom

Dealing with information overload

1 Stop! Be aware of how you feel. Use a relaxation exercise (see page 212) for a few minutes.

2 Be aware of your thinking. What do you see? What do you hear? What do you feel?

3 If you have mental pictures that are moving fast in a blur, slow them down. Change how they look until you are more comfortable.

4 Listen to the sounds in your mind. If there are many voices, just let them die away. If the sounds are loud, turn down the volume. Make them slower if necessary. Change the sounds until you are comfortable with them.

5 Come back to the present moment. Think about exactly what your question is and what is important about that to you. Get the best answer you can right now and know that later you may get a better one.

Choice

NLP has a saying: "If you have only one choice you are stuck. If you have two choices, you have a dilemma. You need three choices for real choice." Choice is good; this is beyond argument. We laugh at the old Soviet Union planned economy in the 1950s and 1960s where you could have any car you wanted, as long as it was a black Skoda. We also assume that if we are deprived of choice, then someone else is hoarding all the goodies for themselves. If three choices are good, then are four better, and five better still?

Europe and the United States are like Disneyworld to someone who lives in a very poor country. Shops full of dazzling goods, things you have only dreamed about, and dozens of varieties of the things you want. Even for people who live there, the choice can be too much sometimes. Once upon a time if I wanted a cup of coffee, I went to a coffee shop and took one of the coffees on the small menu—a few varieties of espresso or cappuccino. Now every time I go, I have choice with a vengeance. First, choose the coffee blend. Do I want Colombian? Brazilian? Kenyan? A mixture? Then, do I want it with ordinary milk, 3% fat milk, 1% fat milk? Cream? Half and half? Hot or cold? And what size: large, larger, or too large? To drink there? To go?

Choice is good, except when there is too much of it. Research indicates that our short-term memory is restricted to between seven and nine pieces of information. Too many choices take us over this limit, so in practice we limit our own choices.

Marketers generally think that more choice is better, so sometimes they bombard us with choices that make it difficult to decide. They assume that the more choices they give customers, the better the customers will like it and the more customers they will get. Some choice is better than none, but more is not better. More and different things do not necessarily make us happier.

Choice and happiness

The gross domestic product of the USA more than doubled from 1974 to 2004, yet the proportion of people describing themselves as "very happy" declined by about 5% (that is, 14 million people). Happiness is subjective; it does not depend on a high standard of living.

Some interesting research asked a large group of people to rate their happiness on a scale of one to ten. A score of one meant they were very unhappy; a score of ten meant Nirvana. The average was 6.5. A lottery win would push the score up to 9 or 10, but a year later the reported rating of the lottery winners was back to an average of 6.5. We adapt to our circumstances. When life improves, we soon take the improvement for granted and expect it. It becomes normal. And then we resent going back to the place where we were content before. The more you have, the more you take for granted and the more you have to lose.

More choice, less value

It also seems that the more choices you have, the less you value what you get. There have been several studies where people were asked to guess the price of a magazine subscription. One group was given one magazine and asked to guess how much it was worth. Another group was given three or four different magazines. The first group, which had no choice, consistently gave the magazine a higher value than the other group with the choice.

When you give people too many choices, you remind them that they cannot have everything. In choosing one thing, they must give up everything else. And as a result, they are less satisfied with the decision they make. They tend to see the opportunity cost, what they have lost rather than what they have gained.

Maximizers and satisfiers

People deal with choice in two very different ways. *Maximizers* are those who aim for the best possible choice in every situation. The more they try to get the best, the more likely they are to regret their decision afterward (when they see they have missed something better). Maximizers see the opportunity cost in their decisions. The more choices there are, the more overwhelmed they become, since they feel compelled to evaluate them all to pick the best.

Satisfiers are people who aim for a "good enough" choice; it does not have to be the best. They don't spend as much time and effort on trying to achieve their goals, or devote as much thought to their decisions. So maximizers are likely to make better choices than satisfiers, yet paradoxically be less happy about them. They get less pleasure from knowing they did well, and suffer more if they discover afterward that they could have done better.

It seems that people with high maximization scores are less satisfied with life and are less happy and less optimistic than people with low maximization scores.

You can easily discover if you are a maximizer. Maximizers tend always to look for the best opportunities, no matter how good life is at the moment. They like to channel surf on the radio and television. They tend to be perfectionists and hard to satisfy. They find it hard to shop for gifts, and also hard to shop for clothing for themselves, as they are always thinking that there could be something better in the next shop. They set high standards and do not easily settle for second best.

Is choice a bad thing? No. Up to a point it's good, and then the psychological benefit tails off. Three choices seem to work well for most people. NLP got it right first time.

Skill for freedom

Dealing with choice

When you want to buy something, narrow your choices to three as quickly as you can. Get help from a friend or someone who knows. You cannot know everything, but you can talk to someone who knows about whatever it is you're buying.

When you make a decision, narrow the field to three options that are acceptable (again, seek expert help if you can). The one you choose does not have to be perfect. Good enough is good enough.

If you find yourself regretting your decision, focus on the good qualities of what you have chosen. There is no perfect choice that has everything; you would have some regret whatever you chose.

None of these things is bad—change, time pressure, information, choice, wanting a better future. How we deal with them makes the difference: they can enrich our lives or make us fearful. There is one more important social anxiety that merits a chapter of its own—pressure to achieve.

CHAPTER 9

The Pressure to Achieve: The Price of Perfectionism

Have no fear of perfection—you'll never reach it.
SALVADOR DALI

WE LIVE IN A CULTURE OF ACHIEVEMENT. All cultures give some people higher status than others. Sometimes this status is *ascribed*, on the basis of education, age, class, or gender. You get status by being who you are; ascribed status does not need justification. In most of Europe and the United States, status is *achieved*. The more you accomplish, the more status you have. Because others tend to judge us on our achievements, we also tend to see ourselves in terms of what we achieve. Our self-image and self-esteem get linked to how successful we think we are, and how successful other people think we are. Success is important. Failure can be humiliating. Failure means loss of status, so we are afraid of failing.

This can cause a lot of trouble. We are not defined by our achievements. We are defined by our *actions*.

There are many forces at work to make us feel that we are not good enough. Advertising is designed to make people feel insecure about everything—their achievements, weight, looks, and social status. The achievement culture encourages people to ask the question: "Am I good enough?" This question provokes anxiety. What if the answer is no? But it is the wrong question. The right question is: "Can I do this to the standard that will get what I want?"

The situation is made worse in a way by the number of self-help books (yes, I know, you are holding one), courses, coaching, and advice available. How can you possibly fail with all this help?

Many people judge achievement by how rich you are. Money is taken as evidence for success. The richer you are, the more successful you are seen to be. This is a ridiculous way to judge success. Many people are very successful in their own field, which may not pay very much. Others do not care about money. And how do we judge who has money? Again, by appearances: big house, big car, expensive holidays. But appearance doesn't say very much about how much money you have. It is possible to have everything financed by loans. Success is not merely about what other people see, but about what is important to you and how you see your achievements.

Self-sabotage

Being afraid of failure is not the same as wanting to succeed. When you want to succeed you focus on your goal. You do everything in your power to get your goal. You marshal your resources, make a clear action plan, and keep track of your progress. In the end, succeed or fail, you have done your best. Fear of failure is the opposite. You lose focus on the goal and instead concentrate on not failing. Your unconscious mind does not process negatives. If you think about *not* failing, you are still thinking about failing, and that is where your attention will be. Self-sabotage follows.

I once coached a very good golfer. He was on the edge of breaking into the "tour" where he could win excellent money. He had talent, but just when he needed a good shot, he would "choke." He described a typical situation where he had to make a good drive off the tee. He knew he had to hit straight. He knew that if he sliced to the left, he would be in the long grass and off the fairway, in the rough. What went through his mind as he approached the shot? He heard a voice in his head repeating: "Don't hit into the rough. Be careful, don't slice to the left." He saw a mental picture of the rough—with his ball in it.

Where was his attention? In the rough. His internal dialogue even gave him instructions on how to get there. The result? He sliced to the left. We worked on his internal pictures and internal dialogue so that they focused on what he wanted, not what he wanted to avoid. This made a big improvement to his game.

What can you do about the fear of failure? Concentrate on what you want. (And don't try to avoid the fear of failure, or you will tie yourself in existential knots!) When you are focused on what you want, there is no room for anything else.

Excuses

Excuses are rife in an achievement culture. Some people make excuses in advance because they count their self-esteem in terms of what they achieve. So they plead extenuating circumstances before they even start. They say in effect that they will "try" but because of the special circumstances, illness, etc., they may not succeed. They have a way out if they fail, and if they succeed, then they perhaps gain even more status because they succeeded against the odds.

It is best to avoid excuses, even if you have good ones; they set you up for failure. They focus your mind on the excuse and make it easier to fail. If you have an excuse, you will probably need it. Tell people about the difficult circumstances and decide whether to make the attempt in advance. If you do go ahead, don't make excuses.

Other people's opinions

How sensitive you are to other people's opinions and feedback determines how much you are affected by the achievement culture. There is another metaprogram pattern in NLP that deals with that: the internal–external pattern. Some people are internally oriented. They decide whether something is good or not. They take other people's feedback as information and decide for themselves. They judge according to their own standards, and their standards are inside them, not given by others. People with the internal pattern know when they have done a good job; they do not need others to tell them. Both internal and external people may be driven to achieve, but for different reasons.

Those with a strong internal pattern may drive themselves hard to achieve. They may not be satisfied with their own achievements, even if others are. They may not care what other people think and just go their own way, doing things in the way they want.

People with a strong internal pattern set standards, they do not follow them. Perfectionism is closely associated with a strong internal pattern plus very high standards; perfectionists usually disregard other people's opinions.

In contrast, people with a strong external pattern get their standards from the outside; they take feedback not as information, but as suggestions or even orders.

Those with an external pattern are more likely to pay attention to cultural messages to achieve, and may drive themselves hard because other people (usually their manager) tell them. Both internal and external people may be driven to achieve, but for different reasons.

Most people have a balance of the two patterns, usually with a slight leaning toward one. They have their own standards, but they are open to feedback from others.

Blame

Everyone is responsible and no one is to blame.
WILL SCHUTZ

The concept of blame is strongly associated with achievement. When success is important, failure needs a reason. The best reason is that someone messed up—*they* are to blame.

Blame is an insidious idea, based on a simplified idea of cause and effect. Under pressure to achieve, blame can be an attractive concept to get us off the hook. But the idea backfires if there is no one else to blame, because then it is *our* fault. A culture of blame is a culture where people are very careful not to step out of line. When there is a strong element of blame in a business culture, the business is usually uncreative, because people are afraid to take chances and they spend a lot of time and effort covering themselves in the event of failure, so that the finger does not point toward them. (This is the classic CYA culture—Cover Your Ass.)

There are three possible areas of blame:

❏ Life's circumstances.
❏ Yourself.
❏ Other people.

Think about how you deal with problems. Is your first reaction to try to see who was to blame, or to blame yourself?

The blame frame

People who are caught in blaming usually ask certain types of questions:

❏ What's wrong?
❏ Who's to blame?
❏ Who's going to fix it?

This is known as the blame frame in NLP—seeing the situation in terms of blame. Blame stops creativity and problem solving. It makes people afraid because when blame is in the air, no one knows when it might fall on them. Blame does not accept excuses. "I didn't mean it" does not absolve you.

The opposite of blame is responsibility. You are responsible for the results you create. You do your best. Often people do not like the word "responsibility" because they think it means the same as blame. But it is very different—it means the ability to give a response. Without this, you cannot take any action and will be powerless.

The contribution frame

> *It is easy to dodge our responsibilities, but we cannot dodge the consequences of dodging our responsibilities.*
>
> JOSIAH STAMP

Blame usually enters when things go wrong. In this case, a better way is to think about *contribution*. No one is to blame, because no one has complete responsibility for what happens. Your success does not depend just on you, but on many people. Instead of blaming, it is better to explore how you and other people contributed to the situation.

Finding your own contribution does not mean that you are to blame, it means that you could have done something different and so you can learn from what happened. Maybe other people had a contribution, and you can understand how and why they did what they did.

When you think in terms of contribution you ask:

❏ How did the other people contribute to this situation?
❏ How did I contribute to this situation?

This is the contribution frame.

Thinking in terms of contribution instead of blame does not gloss over what happened and does not mean that you have to put aside your feelings. The result is the same, but you can learn more. You do not feel as bad, and you escape the fear that comes from a culture of blame.

The outcome frame

Finally, when you have discarded blame and mapped contributions, think in terms of outcomes—what do you want to happen now? Blame always focuses on the past, but you cannot fix the present by considering the past.

The outcome frame asks these questions in the present:

❑ What do I want to happen here?
❑ How can I achieve a satisfactory outcome?
❑ What would it be like if we could solve this problem?
❑ What resources do I have to solve the problem?
❑ How will I feel when I have solved the problem?

Beliefs

Beliefs are habits of thought. We form them from our experience, and they determine the experiences we have. For example, if I believe that I cannot speak in public, I will not try, and therefore I will never get any learning or any feedback about my ability. Beliefs are not true; they are simply our best guesses at reality based on our experience to date. They guide our actions. Our beliefs about ourselves and others stop us from doing many things and therefore from getting experiences that could lead us to question those beliefs. They make the world predictable and therefore we often are reassured when a belief seems to be true, even if we don't like it. "I told you so" is a satisfying phrase to say, even in a disaster.

NLP treats beliefs as presuppositions—assumptions about life, not the truth. They may be wrong, and if we think back, there have been plenty of times when what we believed turned out to be wrong. What is special about your beliefs right now? When you stay open to experience, you will confirm some beliefs and refute others. Limiting beliefs close our minds to experience that might disprove them.

Fear of failure often comes from one of three limiting beliefs:

❑ What you want to do is not possible.
❑ What you want to do is possible, but you are not capable of doing it.
❑ You may be capable, but you do not deserve to succeed.

None of these beliefs can be proved. All you can say is that you have not yet succeeded.

You have to make a leap of faith when you have no experience to back up the new belief. Here is a way to explore the limiting beliefs that are blocking you.

Skill for freedom

Exploring limiting beliefs

---

1 What do you want to achieve? Write this down as a positive goal.

2 What could stop you? Make a list of all the reasons you might not achieve your goal.

3 Look at these reasons. Take them all as statements of belief, not fact. What is the most important and biggest obstacle to achievement in this list?

4 The first step toward overcoming a limiting belief is to put it into words—this separates you from it. So express it as a statement about yourself. Do you believe it? Maybe just a little?

5 Ask yourself these questions about this belief:
   - ❑ How certain are you on a scale of 1–10 of this belief?
   - ❑ Have you always believed this? (Of course not, you were not born with this belief, so what changed your mind?)
   - ❑ What experiences have you had where this was not so?
   - ❑ How would your life be different if you did not believe this?

6 What would you prefer to believe?

   Say what you would prefer to believe. Make this positive, not just a negation of the limiting belief. (For example, if the limiting belief is "I am too weak to achieve this goal," then the positive belief might be "I am strong enough to achieve this goal," not "I am not too weak to achieve this goal."

7 What is the first thing you would do if that positive belief were true?

8 Do it and see what happens!

Failure and feedback

One of the NLP presuppositions states that there is no failure, only feedback.

"Failure" is a judgment—it means that you got a certain result that you did not want to get. People "fail" many times before finally "succeeding." But they might not have ultimately succeeded without the lessons they learned from their failures. A failure could simply be a necessary step on the way to success.

"Feedback" is the results you get so that you can learn from them. Failure is judged to be bad. Feedback is useful.

There are many examples of people using feedback to succeed. Stephen King is one of the world's bestselling novelists. He has sold over 300 million books and has amassed $200 million. Before he had published a single book he worked at a laundromat as a janitor, and then as an English teacher at a school in Maine. He was not well paid. He used all his spare time to write, but publishers rejected all his efforts. One day, annoyed by yet another rejection, he threw the manuscript he was working on into the wastebin. His wife Tabitha pulled it out and told him to keep trying. The manuscript was called *Carrie*. It was eventually published under that title, was hugely successful, and was later made into a film.

Mozart was one of the greatest musical geniuses who ever lived, yet the Emperor Ferdinand told him that his opera *The Marriage of Figaro* was "far too noisy" and contained "far too many notes." Albert Einstein, one of the greatest thinkers of modern times, was told by his Munich schoolmaster that he would never amount to much.

Successful people are willing to fail, over and over if necessary until they succeed. When you think it takes over 1,000 hours of study to become good at any skill, you can see that those 1,000 hours are bound to have their difficult moments. You will go through the phase of conscious incompetence—you know enough to know that you are not very good. Ignorance may be bliss, but incompetence is painful. It can be humiliating. Yet you have to persevere, you have to be wiling to fail many times on the way to success.

Fear of failure

Fear of failure is an unreal fear and there are several ways to deal with it. You can use the relaxation exercise on page 212 to calm fear of failure. Also, fear of failure means fear of loss: an important value is being challenged or you would not care whether you failed or not. So you can also use the transforming fear through values exercise on page 203. You need to discover what mental pictures you are making of failure and then change them, together with the words you are saying to yourself. Finally, mentally rehearse what you want to happen.

When you think about failure you are programming your brain to fail. We bring into reality what we think about.

Here is the main NLP pattern to deal with fear of failure in any context.

Skill for freedom

From fear of failure to action

1 Acknowledge your fear. Relax and breathe freely. You have not failed. Nothing is decided yet.

2 Think about your goal. How are you imagining it? What mental pictures do you have? Look carefully. If you are not aware of any pictures, guess what might be there. It could be you ashamed and humiliated, with "Failure" painted in big letters across your brow. You are right to be afraid of this happening. But it hasn't.

3   Look at your imaginary pictures. If you are associated, then dissociate. Once you dissociate, you will lose most of the fear, it just
becomes a scary movie (or even a comedy).

4   Experiment with the qualities of the picture. This will disrupt the picture and stop it having the same impact. For example, how big is the
picture? Is it colored or black and white? Is it moving or still? Play
with these submodalities (there is a list of visual submodalities in the
resources section).

❑ Make the picture smaller.
❑ Make the picture fuzzy,
❑ Make the picture black and white.
❑ Make the picture like a still photograph.

Some or all of these changes will lessen the impact of the picture.

5   Listen to what you are telling yourself. Listen to your inner voice. If
you are not sure, guess the message you might be saying to yourself.
Here are some possibilities:

❑ "I am no good."
❑ "I will fail."
❑ "They will laugh at me."
❑ "I am not good enough."
❑ "I will make a mistake."

Listen to the voice. Is it your voice? Could it be a parent or a
teacher's voice?

Now experiment with the voice tone. Change the auditory submodalities (there is a list of auditory submodalities in the resources
section). Make it faster. Speed it up so much that it becomes a hyper-
active Disney character. Now make the tone s-l-o-w-e-r. Then make it
so slow that it becomes ridiculous. Now add some funny music. Keep
distorting the voice until you can laugh at it.

What is the positive intention of the voice? What is it trying to tell
you that is useful? Usually, the positive intention of the voice is to

keep you safe, to stop you being ridiculed, or to make sure that you are well prepared. These are good messages. Change the words to express the positive intention and make the message a useful one. For example, you could change "I am not good enough" to "I will be the best I can be."

6   Be clear about your goal. What do you want to happen?

Imagine exactly what you want to happen from a dissociated point of view. See it as clearly and as vividly as you can. Stay outside the experience, watch yourself acting in the situation on a mental screen.

7   Mentally rehearse your goal. When you are satisfied, imagine stepping into the situation and mentally rehearsing (associated) exactly what you want to happen. Be there, seeing through your own eyes and enjoying the good feelings.

8   Anything else? Are there any steps you need to take to make this mental rehearsal a reality?

9   Make an action plan. An action plan is a step-by-step series of actions to attain your goal. You may have to change it as you go along, but you need to start with some structure. In particular, what is the immediate action you can take that will make success more likely?

The frightening pictures were not real. It is far better to think about what you want to happen than what you fear might happen. The first will prepare your brain for success. The second will prepare you for failure. Both are equally realistic.

Performance anxiety

Many people are afraid of public speaking and many professional actors and musicians suffer from performance anxiety even when they have a string of fine performances behind them. Athletes also suffer before a competition. Usually, the more important the performance, the stronger the fear. Some people suffer from excruciating anxiety even at the thought of giving a small speech to a friendly audience who they may never see again.

The first step if you suffer from any sort of performance anxiety is to ask yourself the following very simple question:

Do I deserve to succeed?

You deserve to succeed if you have adequately prepared. If you have not adequately prepared then your fear is giving you a very valuable message. You need to work more on your presentation. For every minute you are in the public eye, prepare for five minutes. If you do not know how to prepare, seek out someone who can teach you or a book that can give you some idea about how to organize your material.

Suppose that you have prepared. You know you deserve to succeed. Yet, the fear still gnaws at you and you cannot understand why you are afraid. You want to succeed, and you know the audience wants you to succeed. (All audiences want to be entertained; they do not want the performer to fail, and they do not want to have to go home after a bad experience, especially if they have paid for it.)

Performance anxiety is fear of the future. If you are adequately prepared and still find yourself afraid of an impending performance, use the following skill that is similar to the fear of failure pattern.

Skill for freedom

Performance anxiety: From fear to action

---

1 Acknowledge your fear. So you are frightened. That is natural. It does not mean that you will fail or make a fool of yourself. The best performers feel frightened before performing.

2   Relax. Breathe deeply and take twice the time to exhale as you do to inhale.

3   What are you imagining? Think about your impending performance. What do you imagine it will be like? What mental pictures do you see? If you are not aware of any picture, guess. It could be of a sea of unfriendly faces staring at you as you forget your speech. It could be you standing looking foolish as people throw rotten fruit at you. You are right to be afraid if this happens. But it hasn't.

4   Dissociate from the picture. See yourself in the picture. Once you dissociate, you will lose most of the fear.

5   Experiment with the qualities of the picture. Play with the submodalities by making it smaller, less clear, taking out the color and the movement (or adding a lot of color and movement). Notice which changes make you feel better.

6   Listen to your internal voice. What are you saying to yourself about the performance? Here are some possibilities:

❏ "I am no good."
❏ "People will laugh at me."
❏ "I should just go home."
❏ "I will look ridiculous."
❏ "Who am I trying to fool?"

Experiment with the voice tone. Make it faster or slower, add music, or make it another person's voice. Use whatever changes you can to feel better.

7   What is the positive intention of the voice? What is the useful message behind the words? The positive intention of the voice may be to stop you being ridiculed, or to make sure you are well prepared. Change the words to express the positive intention and make the message a useful one.

8   Set your goal for the performance. What do you want to happen?

Imagine exactly what you want to happen from a dissociated point of view. See it as clearly and as vividly as you can. Stay outside the experience; watch yourself acting in the situation.

9 Mentally rehearse your goal. When you are satisfied, imagine stepping into the situation and mentally rehearsing (associated) exactly what you want to happen. Be there, seeing through your own eyes and enjoying the good feelings.

Prescribing the symptom

There is one other interesting way of dealing with performance anxiety— deliberately exaggerating the symptom. For example, try to make yourself nervous. If you sweat, try to make yourself sweat more. If your hands are shaking, try to make them shake more. This has an interesting effect. As you try to produce the very thing that is worrying you, it actually diminishes. A lot of the power of these symptoms comes from the effort you make to suppress them. For example, sometimes before I gave a guitar concert, my hands would shake a little. If I tried to stop them, then they would shake more. When I let them shake, they became steady.

Suppose that you are able to increase the symptom. This means that it is under conscious control. If you can increase it at will, then you must have some control over it and you can decrease it—by relaxing.

Another application of this principle is to admit you are nervous before a performance. By admitting it in the open, it can lose its power over you, a lot of which comes from you trying to deny that it is there. What you resist persists.

Metaphors of failure

When you think of failing, what metaphor do you use? Language gives good clues to what is happening and can also suggest the remedy. The language is a metaphor for what is happening to your physiology.

For example, here are some common metaphors that people use to describe failing:

❏ Choking.
❏ Freezing.
❏ Falling apart.
❏ Losing.
❏ Blowing up.
❏ Going down.
❏ Cracking up.
❏ Collapsing.

What phrases come to your mind when you think of failing? All these phrases imply physical tension, so you can tackle your fear by changing the way you use your body. Language gives you a clue about changing your thinking and physiology.

You can apply the following skills at the time (during a performance or an interview or an examination, whatever the challenge you face) or before to combat the fear that might make you less successful than you deserve to be.

Skill for freedom

Changing your physiology

❏ If you think "choking," breathe, relax your throat, and keep your head up.

❏ If you feel you freeze, then relax and imagine a warm glow inside you. Imagine you are standing next to a warm fire. Keep your hands warm.

❏ If you feel you are collapsing, stand up straight; be aware of your body.

❏ If you think of losing, then imagine searching through a treasure trove and finding all the resources you need.

Fear of failure and performance anxiety are unreal fears, but they can be strong enough to stop you succeeding and so become self-fulfilling prophecies. This sets up a vicious circle: the more you fear, the more likely you are to fail and so the more you fear. With these NLP patterns you can break this cycle.

People have been afraid of failure in every country and in every culture. Here is a Chinese story from Confucius, from the sixth century BC.

A good swimmer has acquired his ability through repeated practice—that means he has forgotten the water. If a man can swim under water, he may never have seen a boat before, and still he will know how to handle it—that is because he sees the water as so much dry land, and regards the capsizing of the boat as he would overturning a cart. The ten thousand things may all be capsizing and turning over at the same time right in front of him and it cannot disturb him and affect what is on the inside— so where could he go and not be at ease?

When you are betting for tiles in an archery contest, you shoot with skill. When you are betting for fancy belt buckles, you worry about your aim. When you are betting for real gold, you are a nervous wreck. Your skill is the same in all three cases—but because one prize means more to you than another, you let outside considerations weigh on your mind. He who looks too hard on the outside gets clumsy on the inside.

Pay attention on the inside—don't be clumsy on the inside and you won't be clumsy on the outside. Succeed on the inside and you will succeed on the outside.

CHAPTER 10

Dealing with Change: The Uncertain Future

Our doubts are traitors and make us lose the good we oft might win by fearing to attempt.
WILLIAM SHAKESPEARE

THIS CHAPTER IS ABOUT CHANGE and how to deal with it. Everything changes, but when the change is gradual we do not notice it. Our face does not seem to change from hour to hour, or day to day, sometimes not even from week to week. But compare a contemporary photograph of yourself with one taken a year ago, and you will see a change. We usually accept inevitable and predictable change (although plastic surgery is an alternative to growing old gracefully). More difficult to handle are the changes that are forced on us and out of our control, changes we do not want, or more change than we can handle at one time. The anticipation of such changes can make us afraid. Whatever the change, it takes time. You are on a journey between the present and the future.

We do not notice small natural changes. We notice when they are significant and important enough to disturb our routine and habits of life, or if we gain or lose something important. These significant changes occur in two ways:

❑ They are forced on us and are outside our control.
❑ We decide to make the change.

Both types of change are much easier to handle if we can keep important things about the present situation and take those into the future with us. However, sometimes we cannot.

Change with no choice

Change may be forced on us and be out of our control. Such changes can be very good—a promotion at work or a lottery win, for example. These are not usually a problem, although sometimes they can be stressful. We are conservative when it comes to the good things of life. If these change, we want them to change for the better. Changes we did not choose and perceive as bad are usually very stressful, for example being made redundant, losing money, or having to move house. These changes are disturbing and we fear for the future. Will everything turn out well? Can we cope? Will we be able to have the same good life as we had before?

When you lose your job, there is more than a job at stake—your financial security, your lifestyle, your ability to provide for those you love, even your self-image as a creative, productive person may be under threat. If you enjoyed your work you will lose the daily satisfaction and pleasure you got from it. This change might ultimately lead to something good; for example you might start your own business, be more successful, and have more security and job satisfaction than you had before. Then you would look back on that change and see it as a good one, a challenge that became an opportunity. However, none of this is real at the time when you lose your job. You have only hopes, and they coexist with the fears that you will not find another job, or one that pays much less than the one you lost. The change could lead to depression, illness, and poverty. The challenge would be a nightmare, not an opportunity.

We judge changes as good or bad in the moment they happen, but we can never really know the truth until afterward, sometimes long afterward. The first reaction to unwelcome external change is normally fear and anxiety. We have lost something of value and we are not sure if we can replace it.

The changes we choose

Secondly, we may choose to make the change. We want something better and we then have more control over the change and how quickly it proceeds. Even though there is no guarantee that everything will turn out the way we want, we usually judge these changes as good at the time.

For example, I had a comfortable, secure, well-paid job with excellent career prospects after I graduated from university. I resigned this job after two years to pursue a career in music. I spent two months unemployed before I was able to earn any money. Those two months were frightening, but I never doubted that the change would work well eventually. I never regretted that change, it was right for me.

External and internal change

Change can come from two directions:

❏ In external change, the initiating factor comes from the outside world.
❏ In internal change, the change comes from you.

Changes you choose are always internally driven. No one can force you to make internal changes. Internal changes can be about self-development. For example, you decide to be a more loving person or a more creative person. Internal and external changes go together. Where the change starts is what is important—from an outside event, or from an internal decision? Big external changes will probably develop in you the qualities you need in order to cope. And when you decide to make an internal change, you will seek out helpful people and circumstances, and make a difference to your situation.

Tolerance of change

Some people are more comfortable with change than others. NLP proposes three major metaprogram patterns about how people react to and provoke change. These are preferences, probably built in childhood, and are not fixed for life.

The first pattern is called *sameness*. People with this pattern do not like change and may refuse to adapt to change. These are the people who adopt a new technology or working practice after everyone else (late adopters). They only want a major change every ten years, and they do not usually provoke change. "Don't rock the boat" is a mantra for this pattern.

The second pattern is called *sameness with exception*. People with this pattern like situations to evolve over time rather than change abruptly. They prefer gradual change. They like a major change every five years or so.

The third pattern is called *difference*. People with this pattern like change; they provoke change and resist anything that is too stable or static. They are revolutionary rather than evolutionary. They want major change every one to two years. These people are the early adopters of any new technology. However, they will still resist external unwanted change, although they may deal with it better than people who have a sameness pattern.

You can get an idea about your pattern from the next exercise.

Discovering your metaprogram for change

---

1 What is the relationship between your work this year and your work last year? (If you are not working, then what is the relationship between how you are living this year and how you were living last year?)

2 Think of your main holiday every year in the last five years.

❏ Did you go to a different place each year?
❏ Did you go to the same place each year?
❏ Did you go to the same place until you tired of it and then changed?

3 How many major changes have there been in your life in the last ten years?

4 How many different jobs have you had in the last ten years?

It is easy to see your preference in the answers to these questions.

The *sameness* pattern sees similarities, and your answers will be a variation of "It's the same." You will tend to go to the same place on holiday, have very few if any major changes in the last ten years, and one or two jobs.

Sameness with exception will answer the first question in terms of more of some things and less of others, otherwise basically the same. You will tend to change holiday resorts regularly, have two or three major changes in the last ten years and have done two or three different jobs.

Difference will answer the first question in terms of what is different about work or life (some things will be the same, but this is not what they perceive). Difference people will tend to change holiday resorts every year, have several major changes in their life, and perhaps several jobs in a short period.

This is a rough-and-ready test, it is just meant to give you an idea of your pattern. No pattern is better than another. What is important is to know what you prefer and what you pay attention to. Keep the important things stable. If you have a stable and loving relationship, then you can deal with many other changes.

Major changes

Everyone experiences major changes in their life. These are the most interesting, the most complex, and where we can learn the most. I have a good example from my own experience.

In 2000, I was living in London. I was not very happy with my life, although I was comfortable and successful, I knew it could be better, I knew I could be better, but I did not know how, nor exactly what to do about it. I enjoyed my work—consultancy, training, and writing—but it felt empty. I would sit in my study and stare out the window at the street and let my mind spin on nothing in particular. The leaves on the trees outside the house changed their colors with the seasons, but nothing seemed to change inside me.

I felt as if I were trying to compose a song from only three chords, three chords that came from different keys and didn't even fit together very well. The resulting song varied between flashes of aleatoric brilliance, mere competence, and downright boredom. I wanted a rock song with at least six chords, drums, bass, a mean electric lead, and maybe a soaring saxophone shimmying its way between the silences. I knew that life was not boring; I was bored. I believed I had more than these three chords within me, I believed I could be more, but I did not know how.

Then on a business trip to Rio de Janeiro, I met Andrea and we fell in love. It is easy for me to write that short sentence now, but it cruelly compresses an experience that changed my life profoundly and would take a book longer than this one to do it justice.

I had my life in England and Andrea had her life in Brazil. What to do?

I moved to Brazil.

That's an even shorter sentence that compresses a long and difficult process full of joy, fear, long journeys, late-night telephone conversations, separations, and heartfelt reunions. The decision was easy, but there is a big difference between deciding to do something and actually doing it. Some months had to pass. During that time, I had to make many practical arrangements and deal with an unknown future. My fears were many and varied and mostly to do with losing what I knew, without fully knowing what would take its place.

I had lived all my life in England. I knew English culture; I knew how to behave in England. I knew how to speak English—I took the language for granted and it was my strongest anchor to England, my former life, and English culture. My friends were in England and so were my children. All my habits tied me to England. I valued many things about living in England and the English way of life.

When you are facing change, small things take on an unusual significance. The smell of autumn in England, for example, the chill in the September air, when the leaves are thinking whether to change into brilliant gold, the sun half-heartedly trying to convince you to take an ice cream. The familiar road, the easy walk to the shops, milk delivered every morning, and the high-street shops I knew all gave me the message that life was understandable and thus predictable. My work desk was precisely the way I wanted it with the computer, scanner, and printer all placed exactly where I had placed them. I knew what food I liked and I knew just where to buy it. The magazines that interpreted the world in the way I had become used to were delivered to my doorstep. The newspaper shop was only a block away. I had no idea that I had accumulated so many books and papers, and all of them seemed essential. I was like many people who decide they must throw away some papers to simplify their life or make room for more—I began full of hope and energy, then slowly realized as I went through that *everything* seemed essential. Where to start?

Of course, there were many things about England I did not like. For example, I was glad to lose the English penchant for complaining and the object of so many of those complaints—the weather. I was also glad to be rid of the appalling British cuisine.

I was not afraid of making a new, better life in Brazil. I never doubted that Andrea and I would thrive and be happy in Brazil, and I believed in her and in myself, that I had the resources to make a new, good life with her. However, even this change, which I wanted with all my heart, meant losing many things that I valued.

Loss

This brings us to the essence of fear of change. Fear is based on losing something. Our original fears stem from losing balance (falling) and losing the ones we love and depend on to take care of us (abandonment). Abandonment is the equivalent of death for an infant. The ultimate loss is loss of life. Change means uncertainty, which means we could lose something important to us. We need to come to terms with loss.

Think about the word "loss" for a moment. What images does it conjure up? Most people imagine not just nothing, but a blank space, where something used to be. There is something or someone missing and this brings sadness. We use the word loss as a euphemism for death.

Think now of "losing" something important to you. Most people conjure up an image of having something and then not having it. It's gone. They do not know where it is and they may or may not find it, and they certainly did not choose to lose it. We talk of losing our temper, losing face, losing patience; none of these is fun to do. Losing implies external change with no choice about it.

Now think of "leaving" something rather than losing it. Most people imagine putting something down and moving on. You choose to leave something; it is voluntary, not something that happens over which you have no control. Also, you can go back and take it if you want it again. It is not lost. Andrea helped me see that I did not have to lose anything, I could leave it. The small difference in the word made a huge difference in way I thought about the change.

There are two types of loss. You can lose material things or people, or you can lose experiences. When I moved to Brazil, I left friends and material things I valued, and left the possibility of having certain experiences, like walking up Box Hill in the early autumn and eating Cadbury's chocolate at will. But I can still contact and speak to my friends and the people I love, I still have my former experiences as memories, and I can recall them whenever I want.

My friends and children in England are still a presence. I feel no sadness, and there is no empty space. I did the best I could. I also believe that habits and material things, however good, can hold us back if we cling to them. They should be stepping stones to something better. Beautiful things are a hindrance to a happy life if they trap you. Beauty should point to more beauty. Otherwise, satisfaction can turn to contentment, which turns to indolence, which can lead to stagnation and boredom. You always need a dream beyond the dream you are living right now.

Habits

Habits are closely associated with loss. They are patterns of behavior that we have put time and effort into building. They are unconscious and usually involuntary. Habits keep our world stable. They take effort to build and they take effort to change. It is impossible not to form habits: anything we repeat in the same way becomes easier until we no longer need to devote any thought to it. Habits are bundles of experiences that we have packaged with care so that we always have them.

It is interesting that the word "habit" can also mean an item of clothing, something we put on. It can mean a manner of speaking and doing; people's habits are some of the most characteristic things about them. Habits are what make change difficult because they make life easy in the present.

Some habits we think are trivial were not easy to learn—just watch a small child trying to do up their shoelaces. Habits make life go smoothly, they are very useful—until we want to change. Then they resist and if we identify with the habit, we feel resistant. Habits are always associated with anchors. All our habits have triggers that we are not aware of. The anchors may be something we see, hear, or feel in the outside world or inside ourselves.

You are not your habits because you made them and you can be aware of them. Change always involves becoming aware of the habits you have, stopping some, and learning new ones to replace them.

Habits are hard to inventory, because we are not aware of them. We only become aware of them when something happens to disrupt our life; then we feel uncomfortable because they no longer fit. We only know how much we rely on them when they are no longer there. They open a space in our life and we are faced with learning something new.

Habits pervade our lives; they determine what we do and what we avoid. For example, when I walked the familiar streets of London, I was not normally alert for muggers. I have habits of what I pay attention to as I walk. I pay attention to the traffic because I do not want to be run over. I pay attention to shop windows, but I do not sort out which people are friendly and who might harm me, as the chance of being robbed in the street in the part of London where I lived was very small. In Rio de Janeiro, I needed a new habit—to be aware of the people on the street, particularly when they show an abnormal interest in me. I developed eyes in the back of my head for people acting abnormally. This is similar to the software that scans the way people walk and move at airports. It looks for abnormal patterns of movement, and the police then decide if these constitute a danger.

Habits direct our attention. When something is habitual, you no longer pay attention to it, it becomes background. If habit takes over relationships, how we treat people, and a large part of our work, then we always react in the same way and do the same things. Creativity is lost and life without creativity is dull.

When you want to change, habits bind you like small ropes. The bigger the change, the more habits need to be broken and the more ropes there will be. And they are silken ropes—you can hardly feel them and if you do, they feel comfortable. Most of the bonds are not strong, but the overall effect holds you in place. In *Gulliver's Travels*, the novel by Jonathan Swift, Gulliver is a shipwrecked sailor, washed up on a strange beach. He goes to sleep and when he wakes, he finds he cannot move. The people who live there, the Lilliputians who are only a few inches tall, have tied him down with thousands of little ropes, any one of which he could break easily, but with all of them together he cannot struggle free. This is exactly how habits can tie us down. They give a different, more insidious paralysis than fear.

Change and resources

Any change challenges us to overcome the fear of the unknown future, to deal with losing something we have, and to change our habits. The greatest challenge comes from big changes that we cannot control where we have to change many habits. The more resources we have, the more in control we feel and the easier it is to overcome the fear and change our habits. Any change is a balancing act between two forces: the magnitude of the challenge and the resources we feel we have to deal with it.

When we feel we have more than enough resources to meet the challenge, then we are comfortable. We may even become bored. These sorts of changes are too easy. When the challenge is much greater than our resources, we feel anxious; if it is considerably greater, we will be frightened. We need a balance between resources and challenge. The same principle applies to a good computer game: it needs to be difficult enough to engage the player. If it is too difficult they will give up; if it is too easy they will become bored.

How we perceive the change is crucial. When we do not think we have the resources to meet the challenge then we will be afraid, regardless of what others think.

If we think we have more than enough resources, then we will be complacent and maybe overconfident, even if other people warn us to be careful. Fear is not a problem in the boredom zone. If we are bored, we need to increase the challenge. In the anxiety zone we may be paralyzed and find it hard to act. It can also act as a motivation to go and find the resources we need.

When we are afraid or anxious, we need support. We need friends on the journey who can help us and give us the resources we need. We need people who believe in us even when we do not believe in ourselves. They hold out a helping hand to encourage us to reach a little further than we thought we could. We make an extra effort and so discover that we are greater than we thought.

Rationalization and procrastination

What if we do not get the support or resources we need? Then we may stay tied down by habit, or paralyzed by fear and anxiety. This fear may express itself in different ways.

The first is *rationalization*. We think of all the reasons why we should not move and these seem very compelling. We may be swayed by other people's arguments, paying attention to what they think rather than our own decisions and ideas. This is our fear using another mouth-piece. We make scenarios of the possible bad consequences, and become afraid. We think of many good "reasons" why changing is a bad idea. But reason always serves emotion; we justify what we feel with reason. If we feel afraid, we find reasons to feel afraid. Reason is at emotion's disposal like a faithful old retainer. Sometimes, we pay attention to these fearful scenarios although they are no more reasonable than the good ones. And yet all the time we know in a deeper place than reason can penetrate that the change is right and we want it.

The second way fear is expressed is procrastination. We may delay and delay, thinking that we are not ready. We do not think about how we will know when we are ready. We may set unrealistic standards. (For example, when I am a millionaire, have plastic surgery on my nose, and have visited all the capital cities of Europe, *then* I will be ready to settle down...) Usually we have no way of knowing if we are ready. Procrastination says: "I am not ready. Why not wait?"

The question should be: "Why not now?" There may never be a perfect time for the change, but eventually you have to step off the edge and trust in the support and resources you have.

If you do not get the support and resources you need, you may stay paralyzed by fear, or enmeshed in habits. This is thoroughly frustrating. Either way, it is a vicious circle. You spiral around, wanting to change, but unable to change. All the time the frustration gets worse. Eventually (especially if you are strongly motivated to move away from pain), the frustration can reach a threshold and you are propelled out like a stone from a sling and galvanized to take action.

The fear cycle

The fear cycle is represented in the next diagram.

You start with a dissatisfaction or challenge. You fear you will lose something important, so you stay where you are. Also, your habits keep you rooted in the same place. This leads to frustration and further dissatisfaction. When the frustration builds to a high enough level, you may act. This, as Saruman in *The Lord of the Rings* would say, is the way of pain. It is much better to be proactive and take action.

The fear cycle

You may be afraid of taking the step and making the change, but what is the cost of not doing so?

Use the following skill to clarify what you want.

Skill for freedom

Finding the cost of change

❑ What is the best that can happen if you take this step and make the change? Imagine making the change. What is that like? How important is it to you?

❑ What is the value behind the change? Values help you feel the fear and do it anyway because the result is important.

❑ What is the worst that can happen if you make this change? What is the worst case? What could happen? The worst case is not inevitable. You may decide you can live with this. It is better than where you are now. Or you make plans to deal with these unwanted consequences.

❑ What is the best that can happen if you do not make this change? What is good about life now? Are there reasons to stay where you are besides the risk involved in moving?

❑ How comfortable are you now? What do you value about the present situation? This question will also give you clues about the habits that keep you in place.

❑ What is the worst that can happen if you do not make this change? Could the situation become intolerable? How bad is it now?

This takes us to the next step—what happens once you take action?

Transition

Action takes you out of this vicious circle of fear. Then you come to a very interesting time—transition. You have left the place you were, but you have not yet arrived where you want to be. It takes time to rebalance and stabilize your life.

There is a perfect metaphor for transition in the film *Indiana Jones and the Last Crusade*. Toward the end of the film, Indiana stands high on a ledge, looking out onto a bottomless chasm. He needs to cross it to get to the Holy Grail, which has the power to heal his dying father. He looks across the chasm. It is too far to jump and there is nothing to help him cross, no ropes and no bridges. All he has are faith and trust. So, plucking up his courage, he takes action and steps into space. Then in that marvelous moment, the camera pans to a different angle and you see that he is stepping onto a stone bridge. He *does* have the support he needs. This bridge was there all the time, but it was invisible. He could not see it from the front, because it blended into the rock walls of the chasm. Without taking the step, he would never have known. He throws some pebbles on the bridge to mark it and hurries across to his next ordeal. This is exactly how transition works. There comes a time when you have to step forward, trusting that you will have the support you need.

Another metaphor for transition is the time between one step and the next. Walking is easy once you have learned; yet it involves constantly losing your balance in order to take the next step. You commit yourself in that fraction of a second as your foot moves forward. To stay balanced you have to keep moving. We usually think of balance as static, but static balance is stiff and inflexible. Dynamic balance happens through movement. Think of a tightrope walker. In order to stay balanced, she has to move forward. When she tries to stand still, she will fall. Yet sometimes in the midst of change, this is precisely what we try to do: we freeze instead of moving forward.

Transition is not comfortable. It is ambiguous. We have to keep moving forward, but not too fast. Many people react to transition by trying to get though it as quickly as possible. This does not work.

Transition takes time—and trust.

When you are in transition, you need support. You need someone who can stay with you even in this difficult time, keeping you moving forward. You need to establish new habits; you may need to change some beliefs. And you will learn something new about yourself and others.

Action

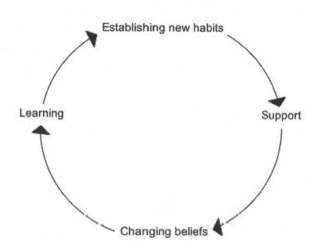

My transition in Brazil took several months. I established a new rhythm of life in São Paulo. I enjoyed the friendliness of the Brazilian people. I watched the purple sunsets over the office blocks and ducked under the blooms of the flamboyant trees on the sidewalk. I began to learn Portuguese, a beautiful language that combines the strength of Spanish with the musical cadences of Italian.

I also saw English culture for the first time in a more objective way. It is impossible to know your own culture while you are immersed in it; it seems *the* way to live, rather than *one* way to live. Once I began to know the Brazilian culture, then my English one became visible by contrast.

Culture is people's collective subjective experience. In NLP, we are careful not to judge individual subjective experience. Everyone has their own map of the world, and you do not try to give them a new, "better" map, but to give them more choices on the map they already have. We need to apply the same to culture. Every culture has evolved ways of dealing with the big questions of life—how to live and survive and how to deal with and understand others. For me it is fascinating to embrace another culture and find other ways of answering these questions. Then, paradoxically, I could appreciate English culture better. Many things that I took for granted in England no longer apply. In Brazil, I can experience the city, the country, and the culture, what people care about and what they don't care about. All around I can feel an intangible sense of style that comes with being Brazilian.

I enjoy living in Brazil. I swim in the warm sea on some of the most glorious beaches on the planet and enjoy the sun. I can make (and drink) Caipirinhas—a blend of ice, lemon, and Cachasa or vodka. When I look up at the night sky I see new constellations and one in particular that I had always thought romantic and exotic, the Southern Cross. The familiar constellations of the northern hemisphere are gone.

I have made new habits of eating, sleeping, and walking on the streets. I am used to the traffic, which snarls the city up for hours a day, and the overfriendly buses that delight in getting really close to you as they jostle their way though the narrow traffic lanes. But it took time and the transition was not always easy.

Experiencing transition

Here is an skill to explore your attitudes to change, and the fears and habits that might hold you in place. It was developed by Andrea, who also developed the transition model. It takes about 20 minutes to complete, but is worth it. At the end you will be much clearer about any change you want to make as well as what helped you make successful changes in the past. It helps to throw some pebbles on the bridge so that you can see it more easily.

Skill for freedom

Transition

Part one: The challenge

Think back to a time when you made a successful change. Do not use a major change for this exercise. (My change to living in Brazil is an example of a very big change.)

The change may have been your choice, or it may have been imposed. It could be predominantly internal (where you changed your character or developed new qualities) or external (a change in external circumstances). Think about the following questions:

❏ What was the change you went through? Describe it briefly.
❏ What was the trigger that led to the change?
❏ Were you dissatisfied with your life in some way and decided to change, or did you have a challenge from the outside that you did not choose?
❏ Was the change predominantly about your internal qualities, or about your outer circumstances?
❏ What fears did you have about the change? (Think back to all the possible bad consequences you imagined, what you were afraid of losing.)
❏ What habits of yours made you resist the change?
❏ What were the important things in your environment, for example people, places, etc. that kept those habits in place?

Part Two: Action

❏ What did you do to make the change? Was there a key realization that made it possible?
❏ What or who supported you? What resources did you need? These resources could be to do with your skills, friends, acquaintances, or your beliefs and values.
❏ What beliefs did you change as a result?
❏ What did you learn?

Part Three: Change now

❑ Now, think of a change that you want to make in the future (internally driven change).
❑ What habits do you have that you will need to change? How do you feel about this?
❑ What fears do you have about the future?
❑ What do you need to believe about yourself that would make this change easier?
❑ How would someone act if they had that belief?

Transition takes time

Change hardly ever happens instantaneously. Transition is part of any change. You need to be ready for it.

❑ Don't expect the change to happen immediately,
❑ Expect to feel uncomfortable for a time.
❑ Gather your resources before you start. In particular, get support from a friend, or a professional helper if the change is a major one.
❑ Keep moving!
❑ Celebrate when you make the change successfully.

When the transition is over, you will have made the change. You will have learned something, left some things, gained others, lost some habits, and established new ones. You will have crossed the chasm. Then, as you walk on, there will be other chasms to cross.

Authentic Fear— Fear as Friend

The nine laws of safety

1 Pay attention to authentic fear.

2 The more you trust your resources the safer you feel.

3 Respect the context, time, and place.

4 To feel safe you need to feel in control.

5 To feel safe you need information that is:
   —Relevant.
   —Sufficient.
   —Trustworthy.

6 Take sensible precautions against possible loss.

7 Have a contingency plan.

8 Pay attention to your intuitions.

9 To stay safe, pay attention to contextual and personal incongruence.

CHAPTER 11

Fear as a Sign to Take Action

The fact that you fear something means that it has not happened.

AUTHENTIC FEAR IS A RESPONSE TO DANGER in the present moment. Its intention is to keep you safe. Authentic fear is evolution's way to ensure that your body is ready to fight, or to run away. It makes you suddenly stronger, more resistant to pain, and more sensitive to what is happening—all useful responses. You cannot decide intellectually to be authentically afraid. The fear response is several steps ahead of your conscious mind; it clicks in before you have figured out what the danger is, or indeed whether there is any real danger at all.

What does authentic fear do for you? It makes you respond, it overrides whatever else you are doing and whatever goals you have, and gives you an immediate and compelling new agenda.

The first law of safety:

Pay attention to authentic fear

Authentic fear is a primary human emotion and an evolutionary mechanism for survival. We cannot live without it. A person without authentic fear would be like a person born without the ability to feel pain. This sounds appealing, but pain is a necessary signal to alert you that something is wrong. Without the ability to feel pain, you could die from appendicitis before you knew you were ill. Without pain you would not know that fire was dangerous. Living without pain could be fatal. Living without fear would be equally dangerous.

Authentic fear is a good ally. It stops you from becoming a victim. People who do brave acts are not fear*less*—the very reason we admire them and see them as brave is because they feel the fear and do it anyway, unlike the usual response, which is to feel the fear and hold back. A person who was truly fearless would not be brave, but stupid.

We want to keep real fear, the fear that warns us that we are in danger. We want to keep the enjoyable fear of action adventures, or horror films, or "white-knuckle rides."

We want to be free of the unreal fear that makes us less than we are, cripples our lives, and is not appropriate to the situation that triggered it. We need to be able to distinguish authentic fear from unreal fear. The next skill will do that.

Skill for freedom

Exploring authentic fear

Think of a time when you were afraid of something real in the present moment, where you had no choice and the fear came up suddenly.

Imagine yourself back there now. See again what you saw. Hear again what you heard and feel again what you felt.

What do you feel?
Where do you have the feeling? In what part(s) of your body?
How large is the area where you feel the sensation?
How deep is it?
How hot or cold is it?
What color does it seem to be?
Does the feeling seem to move or is it still?

Remember these qualities of authentic fear, so that it can be a reliable warning of danger to you.

You need authentic fear

When I hear advice about eliminating fear, it reminds me of the joke about the man who was arguing with St. Peter at the gates of Heaven. St. Peter looks through the book of the man's life and frowns.

"Well," says St. Peter, "I can't see that you have done anything really bad in your lifetime, but that's only the half of it. To get into Heaven, you have to have done some good deeds, and I can't see very many of those here either. If you can tell me one really good deed you did in your life, you can come in."

The man thinks for a moment. "OK," he says, "what about the time when I was coming out of a bar late at night and I heard a girl cry out? There was no one around and I went to investigate. I walked around to the back of the building and there were ten guys harassing a girl. I was furious. The poor girl! I grabbed a piece of wood from the ground and walked up to the leader. This guy was enormous; he must have been over seven feet tall and weighed about 240 lb. He was tattooed all over his arms with slogans I wouldn't dare repeat here. He pulled a knife out from his boot and went into a crouch as his friends formed a circle around us."

St. Peter leaned forward and looked interested.

The man licked his lips. "You want to know what I did? I leapt forward and hit the leader in the stomach with the piece of wood. He didn't even seem to notice the blow! I turned and yelled at the rest of them, as the girl stood cowering next to me. 'You're a bunch of sick animals! Leave this poor girl alone! Go home before I show you the inside of the local Accident and Emergency department!'"

"Really?" asked St. Peter, who was clearly impressed. "When did this happen?"

"About two minutes ago."

The Darwin awards

That man would be a candidate for the Darwin awards. These began over ten years ago as a joke, and now they are awarded every year. They are posthumous awards, named in honor of Charles Darwin, the scientist who first proposed the theory of natural selection—the survival of the fittest. The Darwin awards commemorate people who in the words of the award, "improve the human gene pool by removing themselves from it." They do so because they seem to lack an appropriate sense of fear. Bizarre, sad, and grisly deaths happen every year, in instances where fearlessness becomes stupidity, and the bestowers of the Darwin awards collect the worst and vote on who deserves to win.

For example, the 1990 award went to the incompetent thief who tried an armed robbery in Renton, Washington State, USA. He had no previous convictions, so this was his first and only attempt. He targeted H&J Leather & Firearms, a gun shop. The shop was full of customers, many with guns in their hands. If that was not enough risk, he had to step around a marked police patrol car that was parked outside the front door, which meant it was very likely that an armed officer was inside. When the man entered, the police officer was at the counter drinking a coffee. When he saw the policeman the man must have panicked, because he announced a hold-up and fired some shots, all of which mercifully missed the people inside. The police officer and the shop clerk drew their guns and returned fire, killing the would-be robber immediately. Several other customers had also drawn their guns but did not fire. No one else was hurt.

The most often-quoted Darwin award went to a former Air Force sergeant who was supposed to have obtained a jet-assisted take-off unit (JATO). These are solid-fuel rockets used to give heavy military transport airplanes an extra push for take-off from short airfields. The story goes that he attached it to his car, found a long stretch of road, and started the car—and the rocket. The charred and shattered remains of both him and the car were supposed to have been found four miles away embedded in a cliff face. It is a good story, although it is an urban legend—it never happened.

So fear is there to protect us from danger and harm and it is important to pay attention to it. However, sometimes we are not sure if the situation is dangerous. Sometimes we do not pay attention to our fears or we override them. Fear can only protect us if we act on it, and sometimes we don't, either because we don't notice the danger, or because we underestimate it. How do we know when it is right to act on our fear, rather than ignoring it? We need to calculate the risk involved and to feel safe. These are the themes of the next chapter.

CHAPTER 12

How We Assess Safety and Risk

FEELING SAFE IS THE GREATEST RESOURCE against any type of fear. When you feel completely safe, there is no room for fear. Safety is not some objective ISO 9000 standard; the subjective feeling of safety is what counts and that comes from trust in your resources.

The second law of safety:

The more you trust your resources the safer you feel.

I have just been watching men working halfway up a 24-story building. They are on a flimsy wooden platform, which is lowered on a pulley from the roof. They are wearing hard hats and safety harnesses that are clipped on the pulley wire. They move with assurance and they tell me that they feel perfectly safe. They are used to this life and they trust the equipment that looks so frail to me.

What does safety mean to you?

How do you know you feel safe?

Think of some time when you felt safe, even though there was some threat of danger.

When was that?
What was the risk?

Why did you feel safe?

How did you feel safe? What pictures, sounds, and feelings did you have in your mind?

Think about these questions for a moment before reading on.

Assume risk or assume safety?

Some people assume that events will go well, or at least as expected, unless they get feedback to the contrary. They don't need reams of information before they make a move. For example, I am generally optimistic and assume that things will go well. Consequently, I am sometimes insufficiently prepared.

Other people focus more on the risks in what they do. "Better to be safe than sorry" is their motto. They do not assume success without getting feedback and evidence. They need reassurance that things will go well, so they take many more precautions and gather a lot of information before proceeding. The precautions may be unnecessary, but they need them to feel safe.

Neither pattern is better than the other. Both have advantages and disadvantages, and it is best to be flexible. Look at each situation and take the necessary precautions.

When I drove through South West London late at night, I assumed that I was safe: I did not scan the streets looking for suspicious people. When I drive the streets of Rio de Janeiro, I assume risk. I pay attention to the people around me and how they are acting.

The third law of safety:

Respect the context, time, and place.

What do you need to be safe?

Most people need to feel in control. To feel in control of a given situation you need three things:

- ❏ You need information about the situation.
- ❏ You need to have prepared for the situation.
- ❏ You need to feel you have the ability to deal with any difficult situation that could possibly arise.

The fourth law of safety:

To feel safe you need to feel in control.

Information

The fifth law of safety:

To feel safe you need information that is:

—Relevant.

—Sufficient.

—Trustworthy.

The better the information, the easier it is to predict the future. Too much information is as bad as too little. The best predictions are based on trustworthy information and plenty of it. What makes information trustworthy is the subject of the next chapter.

Here is a personal example about gathering information. Last year, Andrea and I were staying the weekend at a large Brazilian fazenda, which is a cross between a farm and a ranch. This one (as many fazendas do) had a stable with many horses. We wanted to go riding that weekend and here was the perfect opportunity.

Riding is very pleasant, but it can also be dangerous if you get into trouble; falling off a horse onto a rocky road can break your leg or worse. The last time I had ridden a horse had been in Mexico. That had been a wonderful experience riding on a deserted beach—but we had not checked the stables or the horses or the conditions. I fell off about halfway through the ride and hurt my arm. (I got straight back on again!) We had not been to this particular Brazilian stables before and we did not know the people who owned them, or the quality of the horses they had. So we assumed some risk from the start.

Our first impressions were good. There were about three dozen horses, which looked healthy, well fed, and well behaved. The people were friendly and helpful and the facilities were good. The main room had drinks and small snacks and sun cream, and hats were available to borrow if you wanted them. Admittedly these will not keep you safe on a horse, but it showed us that these people had an eye for detail and wanted to make people comfortable, even in the waiting room.

Several children were waiting to go riding and we saw a ride coming back with three children, all of them under ten, swaying happily on top of their mounts and clearly delighted with the experience. All of this suggested that the stable was a good one and it was safe. One of the horses seemed slightly crazy, however. The way it looked around at people reminded me of the psychopath played by Jack Nicholson in the film *The Shining*. It moved in a high-stepping, excited way and looked like it would bolt at any moment. Neither of us wanted to ride this horse, but one man insisted on riding it. We were a little worried, because if this horse bolted, we did not want ours to follow. So we asked the owner some questions:

- ❏ "Are the horses safe?"
- ❏ "Are they well behaved?"
- ❏ "Do any of them bite?"
- ❏ "Do any of them kick if you are behind them?"
- ❏ "Would they bolt if that crazy horse bolted?"

We started with these general questions and then tested the answers with more specific ones. We watched the owner's body language, to make sure he was trustworthy. Our questions were intended to get information, so we could make a decision. (For example, we could also have asked "Have you ever had anyone hurt here?" or "What should we be careful of when riding?")

We did go riding that day. The crazy horse did bolt, but we were ready. I had to keep a tight rein on my horse to stop him following, but we enjoyed the ride overall.

Gather information

Ask questions from different angles. The greater the risk of danger, the more questions you need to ask.

Start with general questions and test answers with more specific questions. If you get an answer that suggests there is danger, ask specific questions to find out about that occasion, what happened, and what were the special circumstances.

Precautions

Safety depends on the precautions you take against danger. "Precaution" is an interesting word. When you do something that could be dangerous, you use caution. Precaution is the caution you use before you start. Caution is taking care. The word "care" has two opposite meanings. When you take care of something you deal with it in a good way. We also say we care about the people we love. However, care can also mean worry. For example, to say "I don't have a care in the world" means that you have nothing to worry about. Worries can be distracting, like wondering if you turned off the gas before going out. Taking precautions before doing something dangerous stops your worries and lets you focus on the task you have to do.

Precautions clear your mind, even if you feel you do not need them. An acrobat without a safety net is at risk, however skilled he is. A rock climber who climbs without a safety harness is taking a big risk: if she makes the slightest mistake, she could die. She may be an expert, she may never have fallen (and of course she does not intend to), but she will feel much safer with safety ropes attaching her to other climbers. Her skill is only one factor. Anything can happen, even to an expert, and anything that can happen will happen, given enough time.

Taking precautions minimizes loss. The more you have to lose, the more precautions you need to take. The less there is to lose, the less you need to take precautions.

When I walk the streets of a dangerous city, especially at night, I take with me only enough cash for what I am planning to do, and one credit card for emergencies. Then if I were to be robbed I would not lose so much.

The sixth law of safety:

Take sensible precautions against possible loss.

Contingency planning

You take precautions to avoid the risk of something going wrong. But suppose it does? What then? Your safety also depends on whether you can *deal* with something going wrong. How can you prepare yourself for the worst? When you know you can cope with the worst that life can throw at you in the situation, then you will feel safer about taking the plunge.

There are many examples of this. The first thing a martial arts teacher will show you is not how to hit someone, but how to take a hit, and how to fall. When you learn canoeing, the first thing they teach you is what to do if you capsize. If you are serious about taking up horse riding, then your teacher will show you how to fall off a horse without hurting yourself.

Planning for the worst case is not negative thinking. It is positive and helpful. You take precautions beforehand of course, but you will be extra confident when you know that you can cope with emergencies, even while hoping that they will never arise.

Insurance companies make money from this principle. Insuring yourself against injury does not make it less likely that you will injure yourself, but it does cover you if you do.

Making a will is another example. No one wants to die, but if you die without a will, then it will be difficult for your loved ones to sort out the finances and it usually means that the government gets an unfair share. Yet, many people do not make a will because they feel that it brings death closer.

Having a BATNA (Best Alternative To Negotiated Agreement) in a negotiation is a third example. You cannot assume that there will be an agreement, so you need to know in advance what you will do if the negotiation breaks down completely.

You cannot plan for every contingency. There is usually only one way for things to go right, but an infinite number of ways for them to go wrong, just as there are more ways for a room to be untidy than tidy. Plan for important contingencies, where there is a greater than usual risk, or where the risk may not be great, but the consequences would be devastating.

The seventh law of safety:

Have a contingency plan.

There are three ways to prepare for eventualities:

- ❏ *Prepare a plan.* Sometimes this is enough. What will I do if the deal falls apart? What will I do if I don't get the job?
- ❏ *Mentally rehearse.* Decide what you will do in advance and imagine doing it in detail. This technique is crucially different to worrying. Worrying is thinking "What if this happens?" and then agonizing over that imagined scenario. Mental rehearsal is about action and prepares you for the worst.
- ❏ *Physically rehearse what you will do.* This is important when what you are doing involves physical skill, for example horse riding or martial arts.

Risk

A ship in harbor is safe—but that's not what a ship was built for.

Contingency planning brings us to the idea of risk. Risk is the possibility that something dangerous will happen. When we are at risk we are afraid, and we can manage our fears by managing risk. Risk management maximizes the areas where we have some control over the outcome and minimizes those where we have no control.

There are four elements in risk

❏ *Our resources.* What do we have to lose?
❏ *The probability.* How big a probability is there of winning or losing?
❏ *The stake.* What is at stake? What do we stand to lose or gain?
❏ *Our values.* What is important to us? How much do we value a win? How important is the loss?

Our resources influence the risks we take. A rich man might risk $1,000 on a spin of the roulette wheel. The odds against him winning are large, but if he does win, he wins the jackpot. The highest probability is that he will lose his stake. Does he care? Not if he can afford to lose $1,000 and he probably only wants to play for high stakes. He has to take a bigger risk of losing if he wants the chance to make a lot of money. This is how a rational rich man might behave, but he may have his own agenda. He may gamble just for the thrill of it. He may be greedy for more money, even in (to him) small amounts. He may be testing his gambling method and so on. So we cannot talk about risk in the abstract, there has to be a risk taker, with their own values, beliefs, and motivations.

Risk aversion

We say that people are risk averse, but more accurately they are *loss* averse. Loss is painful. The possibility of loss is what adds danger to risk and this makes us afraid, so we are willing to pay for peace of mind, even when mathematically the odds are against us. For example, we pay our insurance premiums because we prefer to have the certainty of a small loss (the premiums) to avert the (small) possibility of a large loss (injury, fire, robbery, flood, etc.).

We do not act rationally about risk. We see the risk of loss more strongly. Loss is behind all fear. We hate to lose. Consider this experiment, published by Kahneman and Tversky in 1984.

They proposed that a rare disease has broken out in the community and it is expected to kill 600 people. There are two possible plans to deal with the threat:

❏ Plan A—200 people will definitely be saved.
❏ Plan B—there is a 33% probability that everyone will be saved and a 67% probability that no one will be saved.

Which would you choose? Choose one plan before reading on.

Rationally Plan A has to be better and 72% of people they asked chose this option.

Now they posed the problem differently: the same disease, with two new programs:

❏ Plan C—400 people will definitely die.
❏ Plan D—a 33% chance that no one will die.

Now 78% of the same respondents went for Plan D. They could not take the loss of 400 lives. I wonder if the figures would be different if they were told that they were part of the community, rather than an outside observer.

Rationally, of course, the two problems are identical. This experiment makes it clear that our decisions are influenced by the way they are posed—whether the loss or the gain is in the foreground. Advertising, opinion polls, and referendums use this principle.

Costs and losses are the same in accounting terms, but we tend to value them differently. We may tolerate something if we see it as a cost, but not if we see it as a loss.

One professor of finance has a good strategy to help him deal with small losses. At the beginning of every year, he sets aside a generous donation to his favorite charity. Whenever anything bad happens during the year—he loses money or has to pay a fine, for example—he charges it to his charity account. Then he feels better because he has not lost it, the charity has. At the end of the year, the charity gets what is left over, The perfect, self-interested philanthropy strategy!

We also tend to pay more attention to dramatic and unusual events than to routine events. We remember them and they sway our decisions and our choices in taking risks.

There is a good joke that nicely illustrates this. Three heads of state are talking together at a United Nations reception. One is the head of a powerful and aggressive state, the second is his ally, and the third is neutral.

Powerful is talking about his invasion plans for a small country. He says to Neutral, "We are send in our troops next week. We will kill about 2,000 peasants and three chiropodists."

"Neutral replies, 'What! Why on earth are you going to kill three chiropodists?'"

Powerful turns to his ally and says, "See, I told you no one would care about the peasants."

Ambiguity aversion

In practice, we evaluate risk every day based on the probability of loss and the seriousness of the consequences. We put the two factors together and come to a decision based on what we perceive to be at stake. The more uncertainty, the more risk. The more risk, the more possibility of loss. Also, we usually tolerate familiar risks over strange ones, so we may judge something a bigger risk if we are unfamiliar with the situation. This is known as "ambiguity aversion."

So a working definition of risk is:

Risk = the perceived danger of loss, evaluated from:

❑ The perceived probability of loss.
❑ The value of the possible gain.
❑ The seriousness of the loss.
❑ How familiar the situation is.

Here is an example to illustrate. A few weeks ago, I was a guest at a wedding that was held on a country farm. There were wonderful walks all around and a small river went through the land. A group of us walked down to the river through some shady paths that hid hundreds of multicolored butterflies that flickered through the trees like small flames, until we came to a place where we could bathe in the river. The sun was shining and the river was clear, no more than waist high but very cold. A little way upstream there was a small waterfall where some large rocks blocked the flow of the current and a tree had fallen across the stream. The rocks and branches formed natural rapids. Further upstream the water was calm again. It was the perfect adventure playground for adults.

A group of us went into the water and clambered over the rocks that were blocking the stream. They were slippery and mostly overgrown with moss; many were sharp, especially under the water. The fallen tree provided some handholds, but it also contained a number of suspicious-looking spiders. Disturbing Brazilian spiders is not a good idea, since they can give you a nasty bite.

I moved through the rocks, jumping from one to the other, taking care and judging what was possible, until I reached a comfortable one in midstream. The sun was high by this time, I was hot, and I had forgotten to put on sun lotion. I saw a rock in the shade over to the side of the river and decided to try to get there. It meant a jump; there was no other way. I gauged the distance and thought I could probably make it, but the stones were slippery and if I did not make it cleanly first time, I risked falling into the rocky water, cutting and bruising myself badly, and at worst breaking a limb. I estimated that the probability of failure was about 30%, and I gave a high figure (say 70%) to the seriousness of the consequences. I did not jump in the end, because it was not very important to me to get to that rock, there was plenty of easier shade to use, and I did not want to spend my holiday in hospital.

Andrea was following me across the waterfall and I went back to help her. She crossed and after sunning ourselves a little we went back, carefully avoiding disturbing the spiders.

Talking with her afterward about her experience of climbing through the rapids to the rock where I was, she thought that her probability of failure without help was 60% and the consequences of failing were the same as mine—bruises and possible broken limbs (70%). She saw a higher risk than me and she did not want to do it without help. Help reduced the probability of failing and also reduced considerably the seriousness of the consequences, so it made it a reasonable risk and she went ahead because it was important to her.

Risk is a subjective concept. Everyone has to decide the probability of loss for themselves and also give a figure to the seriousness of the consequences. It depends how the risk is made up. If the consequences are very serious, then you may not take the risk even if you are reasonably sure of succeeding. You would only take the risk if the probability of failure were zero. (This is a special case because there is then zero risk.) On the other hand, if the consequences are not at all serious, then you may take the risk even if you think you have very little chance of success; after all, you have nothing much to lose.

Risk does not come down to cold-blooded, mathematical probabilities. You assign the values, and you will suffer the consequences; risk has an emotional value as well as a mathematical one.

Your values do not change, so to reduce a risk you must either reduce the seriousness of the consequences (in my example the seriousness would have been less if I had been wearing protective clothing) or increase the probability of success. The value can sway the balance. Someone may risk high consequences with little chance of success if it is very important. Andrea did negotiate the rapids.

The risk may be high, but if the motivation is high, we will take the risk anyway.

Skill for freedom

Checklist for risk

You want a change and this means taking a risk. You can evaluate the risk with this checklist.

1 What is your estimate of the probability of your failing to get what you want?

2 What is your assessment of the consequences of failure?

3 What is important to you about the possible gain or loss?

4 How can you decrease the risk by:
   ❑ Decreasing the seriousness of the consequences of failure?
   ❑ Getting a higher probability of success?

5 What resources do you need that will give you a higher probability of success?

6 Can you trust these resources?

7 What reference experiences have you had in the past that give you confidence in these qualities?

8 How important is the change you want to make?

CHAPTER 13

Acting on Fear:
When to Heed the Warning

How do you know when to act on your fear?

Sometimes it is obvious. There is immediate, physical danger to yourself or your loved ones. You get the full biochemical jolt and you are ready for action—fight or flight. For example, someone jumps out at you in the dark, or a crazy driver pulls in front of you on the motorway. You do not have time to think or agonize over what to do; you react quickly and often surprisingly calmly, considering the hormonal ferment in your body, although you may shake with fear afterward.

Because authentic fear normally makes you react without thinking, there is a danger that you will do the wrong thing—if you have learned the wrong thing. For example, I once lost control of my car on a wet road and started to skid. I had never been in a skid before, so I tried to compensate by turning the car in the opposite direction to the skid. This seems the obvious, commonsense thing to do. The car goes one way, turn the wheel the other way. Of course, this is the wrong thing to do. It makes the skid worse, and now I know this from personal experience. The car finished upside down in the middle of the road. I was unhurt and crawled out of the broken rear window. I knew in theory what to do: turn into the skid. I even thought of that when I was skidding, but my hands just would not do it. I did not believe it at the crucial time. If I had practiced getting out of a skid, even once before, I am sure I would have done the right thing. Sometimes it is not enough to *know* what to do in theory, you have to practice it, if not physically, then mentally.

Warning signals

Most of the time, however, situations are ambiguous. Sometimes you should be afraid, but do not notice the warning signs. Here is an example from my experience.

I have spent a lot of time in Rio de Janeiro, one of the most beautiful cities on the planet, perched on the Atlantic coast of Brazil and blessed with some of the world's best beaches. Rio is a tourist magnet, set as it is on the slopes of purple mountains that drop down toward the Atlantic. Flying into the international airport you see a view that you will never forget.

Rio has unparalleled nightlife, wonderful restaurants, and a hedonistic culture that pursues pleasure with enthusiasm. Christo Redentor, the huge granite statue of Christ, looks down on its inhabitants from the peak of Corcovado with his arms open and accepting. Few cities can boast such a beautiful setting.

But Rio has another side to it, as I have already mentioned. Many parts are dangerous. The majority of the people who live in the city are very poor. Many live on the streets and many more live in favelas, enclaves that are communities in themselves. These have their own laws, enforced by the most powerful people who live there—usually drug dealers and people involved in organized crime. You never enter a favela unless someone who lives there accompanies you.

Driving in Rio is both alarming and confusing, so you can easily drive into a favela without realizing it. There are several all over the city, some very close to the most fashionable tourist areas. Tourists have more money than the locals, so the very rich and the very poor rub shoulders on the streets and beaches. A wristwatch, which would be a trivial purchase of utilitarian value to a tourist, would represent a month's food to a poor Carioca.

I was walking back to my hotel in Copacabana one evening with Andrea; there were several people on the street at the time, both in front and behind us. Suddenly Andrea stopped and whispered, "Just a moment." I was not frightened; I did not know why she had paused. She had seen two men behind us and when we stopped, they continued to walk past laughing. We pretended to talk and we saw them stop a little further on. We turned back and went into a small flower stall at the side of the street. They followed us in. By that time, I was frightened. The stallholder of the shop was too, it looked like he recognized our followers and did not like what he saw. We pushed past them quickly out of the shop, made a sharp turn, and crossed the street, losing ourselves in the crowd. We walked fast in the opposite direction. I was not frightened until I was in the flower shop, but if I had been alert, I would have seen the two behaving suspiciously and felt frightened earlier.

Danger signals can be ambiguous; much depends on the context (the third law of safety). Rio is a more dangerous city than most and these two men were clearly giving signals that I did not notice, but Andrea did. I learned my lesson—be alert to my surroundings. I did not appreciate the dangers of Rio at the time and thought that I was safe on a crowded street. People who live in Rio will tell you that having people around you will not guarantee your safety.

Denying fear

Often we may feel afraid, yet discount our fear or logically try to argue that there is nothing to fear. When a stranger starts up a conversation and we suddenly feel afraid for no obvious reason, what do we do?

Denial of fear can make us victims in many situations. Sometimes fear surfaces as an intuition: there is no real evidence, but we know something is wrong, although it is hard to put our finger on it exactly. Our intuition is picking up signals from beyond consciousness.

Always pay attention to your intuition. The root of the word is the Latin verb *tuere*, which means to guard or protect. We may discount those fears for many reasons: we want life to go smoothly, or we care about what others think about us and try to avoid the ridicule and embarrassment of crying wolf. We want to think the best of others to avoid hurting their feelings or being made to look stupid. We are brought up to trust people and life is easier if they are trustworthy.

(Notice the interesting double meaning to the English phrase "perfect strangers." It can mean both someone we do not know and a stranger who has nothing wrong with him or her.)

Sometimes we dismiss our intuition when we should be paying attention to it. We read in the papers that there are muggers, robbers, and assorted psychopaths out on the streets, but surely none of those are people we know. People we know get the benefit of the doubt. But when a Jekyll and Hyde acquaintance suddenly goes berserk and is arrested, local people will often say, "I knew there was something funny about him..." Some may say this to appear knowledgeable after the event, but many people do have an intuition long before any trouble occurs. We are very sensitive to the way other people behave, what they say, and the kind of "vibrations" they give out. Our normal senses of seeing, hearing, and feeling are far more acute than we usually give them credit for; we do not need any sixth sense.

The eighth law of safety:

Pay attention to your intuitions.

Predicting violence

We may get warnings of violence, which can be predicted by the same skill we use to understand people—the universal human talent of empathy. We are capable of feeling every emotion under the sun, and have felt them all at one time or another. We run through the entire gamut of emotions in childhood and we remember them all. This allows us to recognize similar emotions in other people. Children feel keenly and their emotions fluctuate; they can feel murderous rage and unconditional love in the same afternoon. As we mature, we learn to control our emotions and transform negative emotions, without having to act on them.

Violence does not spring out of nothing; it is always preceded by a thought. Thoughts are not confined to the brain: they become visible though words and body language, even if the person is trying to mask them. When the thoughts are charged with emotion, they show in the body. We can usually see if someone is angry even if they are trying to hide it: it leaks out in their posture, tonality, and expressions. The more you know the person, the easier it is to see.

There are universal signals of body language that precede violence. These signals stay constant from culture to culture. Desmond Morris, an ethnologist who has studied crosscultural non-verbal expression, lists 66 body language signals that are constant in every culture. Many of these are unconscious. Many we can pick up without knowing exactly how we do so, but we respond to them.

For example, a stranger comes up to you in the street and asks what time it is. He is well dressed and smiles as he asks. This seems a harmless situation. Yet you may feel threatened. Why? He is only asking what time it is, why think ill of a perfect stranger?

What do you do? Maybe nothing. Maybe you retreat a pace and quickly glance at your watch.

What sort of signals could you have picked up without realizing that gave you the intuition of danger? Here are some possibilities:

❏ He had just passed a big public clock, so why did he ask you the time?
❏ The man smiled but there was no warmth in the smile, his eyes stayed cold.
❏ His shoulders were tense and he was standing a little too close to you for comfort. He looked behind him just before he asked you (checking that the coast was clear for a getaway?).
❏ He smelt anxious. Smell is one sense that we do not use consciously. We are taught from childhood not to notice smell, or if we do to say nothing. It is considered very impolite in many cultures to comment on how a person smells. There is a multi-million-dollar deodorant industry designed to block out any smell that is remotely natural. Yet people do give out smells. We talk of

the "scent of fear," we say that something "smells dangerous," or that the situation "smells wrong." These are more than mere metaphors. When someone is anxious, or frightened, or stressed, the biochemical changes in their body will change their smell. We may pick this up unconsciously and we have learned to disregard it, so the information comes in another way—by intuition.

With this information, it would be sensible to look the man directly in the eye, point to the public clock, and then walk very quickly and resolutely in the other direction.

Danger signals

There are some other signals of personal danger to pay attention to if you see them. The key to these is *incongruence*. A person is incongruent when the signals they give out are not consistent. Two types of incongruence may spell danger:

❏ The first is *contextual* incongruence, when a person's words or actions do not fit the context. This can be harmless, for example a business meeting where the presenter is wearing a T-shirt and trainers; or a restaurant where the waiters ignore you (unless you are in France, when it is perfectly normal). Other signals are not so harmless, like a stranger who insists on seeing you to your home, when you clearly decline the offer, or a work acquaintance who starts sending you unusually friendly letters and standing in the street outside your house at night.

❏ The second is *personal* incongruence. This is when a person's actions and words do not give a consistent message in the context. Of course, no one is completely congruent all the time: civilization demands that we sometimes hide our feelings. We may say that we will do something, but fail to do it, for example. However, certain types of personal incongruence can often spell danger, like friendly words accompanied by a predatory smile, or any smile that does not touch the eyes, or friendly words with clenched fists.

The ninth law of safety:

To stay safe, pay attention to contextual and personal incongruence.

Some personal incongruence signals are always worth paying attention to, especially if they are also contextually incongruent.

The first is "forced teaming." This is when someone starts to use "we" instead of "you" or "I." They say things like "Let's get this done" or "We can't let that happen, can we?" They force an alliance with you without a good reason. Forced teaming acts as a kind of reassurance—"Hey, we are in this together..."—but why would you need reassurance, unless there was a threat? Forced teaming is designed to make you drop your guard.

The second signal comes from unnecessary details and explanations. When people tell the truth, they do not doubt themselves. When they lie, it may sound credible to you, but not to them—they know it is a lie, so they bolster up the explanation to the point where, to quote Shakespeare, "Methinks he doth protest too much." When someone gives too much explanation, they may be more interested in convincing you of their story than in making a genuine proposal. A promise that you did not ask for is another signal of a similar nature. Why would they want to promise you, unless there was some doubt? A statement would be enough.

The third signal is trying to put you under a sense of obligation by offering unwanted help. If you need help it is always better to choose someone yourself and ask directly. Some people are naturally helpful, but then they will not press their help on you if you say no. Enforced help is designed to make you feel in someone's debt, so that you are more likely to go along with other proposals they may have.

The attribution error

These sorts of approaches rely for their effectiveness on what psychologists call the "fundamental attribution error." This means ascribing to identity what is really behavior. If someone acts in a charming way, we tend to think of them as a charming person. They are not: they just acted in a charming way.

NLP makes this distinction through the structure of neurological levels, as elaborated principally by Robert Dilts. There are five levels:

❑ The first level is the *environment*—the place, the time, and the people involved. The environment sets the context. Environment looks the same to everybody who is there.
❑ The second level is *behavior*—our actions. Behavior is visible from the outside.
❑ The third level is *capability*—our skills, both physical and mental. Skills make us behave in ways that are consistent, automatic, and habitual. Capability is not visible from the outside; we cannot see the capability itself, only the results in a person's behavior.
❑ The fourth level is *beliefs and values*. Beliefs are the principles that guide our actions, not what we say we believe, but what we act on. Values are why we do what we do. They are what are important to us—the things we pursue—health, wealth, happiness, and love. Beliefs and values are not visible, except in behavior. Our beliefs and values tell us what to do, our skills allow us to do it, and our behavior is the observable result.
❑ The fifth level is *identity*—our sense of ourselves, our core beliefs and values that define us and our mission in life.

Neurological levels are not a hierarchy. They all connect to each other and all influence each other. Identity is not the "highest." In fact, there is good evidence that identity changes under extreme environments and circumstances (for example prison). Identity is not a stable, identifiable set of traits but a bundle of habits (capability) and beliefs that are dependent on context. The reason that identity stays stable is because we are so good at controlling our environment.

Now from the inside point of view—from our perspective, we express our identity, beliefs, and values through our behavior. From the outside, people see behavior, not identity. When we look out for danger, we need to look at behavior and context, not identity. We know nothing of a person's identity apart from what they tell us by their actions. Their actions give clues to a person's intentions. If we confuse behavior with identity, we tend to attribute qualities to people that they may not have. What matters is intention, and this is invisible from the outside.

Rapport is not enough

Many people are very good at building rapport—a sense of relationship and trust. Rapport can be built at all the neurological levels.

Rapport at the level of environment is how we dress and appear. We tend to be well disposed toward people who look like us. If someone approaches us in the street dressed in rags, we might be immediately suspicious that they want money. A well-dressed stranger looks respectable. It can be important to get rapport on the environmental level (for example, wearing a suit to a business meeting and not jeans), but it is not a reliable indicator of good intention, because it can be so easily manipulated. Confidence tricksters always make sure that they look good, fit in, and meet expectations.

Behavior can also be manipulated. Rapport is built on the behavioral level by matching voice tone and body language, and this is something that NLP has studied extensively (see *The NLP Work Book* in the list of resources for details). Matching body language is something we do naturally: we tend to match eye contact and general posture with those to whom we talk. We also tend to match our voice tone—we speak more softly if the other person has a soft voice, and we match the other person's speed of speech.

There is good research dating from the 1960s by William Condon, who looked at what he called "cultural micro rhythms," the repeating patterns in communication behavior. What he found (which has been confirmed by subsequent researchers) was that gestures and voice rhythms tend to harmonize when we talk to another person. The volume and pitch of the voices equalize and so does the speech rate (the number of speech sounds per second). The latency period also equalizes (the time that elapses between one person stopping talking and the other beginning).

You can get rapport by deliberately matching body language and voice tone. If you do it too much, it becomes mimicking, which is usually very offensive. Since body and voice matching is a learned skill, this can also be manipulated by people who may want rapport with you but with a bad intention. Trust and intuition are the most reliable guides to safety. These are considered in more detail in the next chapter.

Skill for freedom

Danger signals

Forced teaming.

Unnecessary details and explanations.

Creating a false sense of obligation.

Contextual incongruence, when the behavior does not fit the context.

Personal incongruence, when the body language is incongruent.

Your intuition makes you feel uncomfortable.

CHAPTER 14

Trust and Intuition: Your Two Guides

TRUST IS THE MOST IMPORTANT ELEMENT OF SAFETY. If the mountain climber does not trust the rope that supports his weight, he will not feel safe. We also need to trust ourselves and our resources in the event of danger.

The word "trust" comes from the Old Norse word *traustr*, meaning "strong." The word "true" comes from the same root. You trust something when you know that it is strong enough to bear your weight, in reality or metaphorically. The feeling of trust is a mixture of confidence, strength, and safety that is based on experience—more than hope and less than certainty.

Level of trust

Your level of trust depends on two things: how much weight you put on the support, and its strength. If you don't lean hard it does not need to be very strong, but if you are going to trust it with your full weight it needs to be stronger. Some people are trustworthy up to a point but then fail under pressure. You might trust a person with $50, but not with $1,000. You may trust a friend with your credit card, but not with your boyfriend.

Trust is not an all-or-nothing quality—there are degrees. It is not about accounting and adding up the positives and negatives surrounding a person, it depends on context.

Skill for freedom

What does trust mean to you?

This exercise gives you a way you can measure trust.

Think of a time when you successfully trusted someone.

What are the qualities of the feeling?

- ❑ Whereabouts in your body do you experience it?
- ❑ What temperature is it?
- ❑ How deep is it?
- ❑ What area does it seem to take up?
- ❑ Is there anything else important about it?

What picture do you see?

- ❑ What are the qualities of the picture, regardless of what or who is in it?
- ❑ How big is the picture?
- ❑ Are you in the picture, or are you looking at yourself in the picture?
- ❑ Whereabouts do you see the picture (front, left, right, up, down, etc.)?
- ❑ Is the picture in color or black and white?
- ❑ How far away is the picture?
- ❑ Is the picture moving or still?
- ❑ Are there any other important qualities of the picture?

What sounds do you hear?

- ❑ Is there an internal voice?
- ❑ What does it say?
- ❑ What message is it trying to give you?
- ❑ Are there any other important qualities of the sound?

Make a list of these qualities. Write them down. **Save them.**

This is a precise representation of how you experience trust. When you are uncertain whom to trust, think about the person and see how far your images, sounds, and feelings measure up to this benchmark.

Three types of trust

There are three main categories of trust:

❏ Trust in your environment.
❏ Trust in other people.
❏ Trust in yourself.

Trust in the environment

Trust in the environment is simple. Ask questions and test as much as you can. You test if a rope is strong enough to support your weight by putting more weight on it that you would ever expect it to carry. If it holds, then you have a good safety margin.

All the information (or at least the important bits) has to match up and point in the same direction before it is completely trustworthy.

Trusting others

Trust in other people is more complex. There are four elements to trusting others:

❏ Sincerity.
❏ Congruence.
❏ Consistency.
❏ Competence.

You trust someone if they are sincere and truthful. They mean what they say, they deliver what they promise. But do they do this only if they are feeling good? Only if they can get something for themselves?

We judge people's sincerity by their facial expression, body language, and voice tone. When someone is sincere, they are telling the truth, as they know it. (They may be mistaken, however.) When we do not think a person is sincere, then we do not trust them. They do not have to be a "good" person for us to trust them—criminals may be very trustworthy in certain circumstances.

The second element is congruence. In practice, we judge a person's sincerity by how congruent they are. They are congruent when their words and actions match up. Congruence means a strong voice tone, looking you in the eye, symmetrical body language, and the words "Yes I will!" When we see these, we normally judge that the person is sincere and telling the truth (although they may have mastered the art of congruent lying). We do not think they will trick us.

In practice, few people are completely congruent. They may be uncertain, or they may not be feeling well. If we notice that a person is very incongruent, then we do not usually trust them. Congruence also applies to information.

The third element of trust is consistency. Most people need to know another person for some time before trusting them. Others need to see that they keep their promises on a number of occasions, regardless of time. Usually if someone is trustworthy on three occasions, this is good evidence that they are generally trustworthy. Someone who keeps their promise one day and breaks it the next is not trustworthy; next time there is a 50% chance that they will break their promise again.

A person may be sincere, and congruent, and consistent, but can they do what they say they will do? You would not trust a six-year-old child to operate an electric saw without supervision, however sincerely they pleaded that they wanted to help you.

Competence is much more important than confidence. Confidence is the feeling that your resources are as great or greater than the challenge you are confronted with. Confidence needs to be grounded in information, trust, and competence. Misplaced confidence leads to trouble. (Would you rather be operated on by a confident or a competent brain surgeon?)

Many people will sincerely offer to help you, but not know how, or may not have the skill. When someone can help you and lets you down, this is worse than when someone sincerely tries to help but is unable to because they do not have the resources. They are incapable rather than untrustworthy. The specific situation is very important. A trustworthy person must be consistently sincere, congruent, and competent in the same context.

Thresholds of trust

People have different thresholds of trust. Some people never trust others. They are always suspicious and reluctant to trust anyone else in finances, relationships, or business. These people may lose a lot of opportunities and fun in life. Other people trust too readily: they treat people as generally trustworthy without gathering much evidence. They may just like someone and trust them immediately without checking further. This can be dangerous and such a person may experience a lot of disappointment. They might flip after a few bad experiences, and decide that no one is trustworthy and refuse to trust anyone.

Always trusting people and never trusting people come from the same source—not paying attention to people. We need to pay attention to the other person's congruence, sincerity, and competence over time before deciding to trust them.

Trusting another person is a wonderful feeling and having that trust returned is the basis of the happiest relationships. The exercise on what trust means to you (page 174) gives you a benchmark to measure the trust you have for different people. Or try the skill below.

Skill for freedom

Exploring trust

How do you decide whom to trust?

How do you decide when to trust?

What rules do you have about whom you trust?

What do you look for and listen to in a person in order to trust them?

What evidence do you need to trust someone?

Trusting yourself
Trusting yourself follows the same logic as trusting others.

❑ How sincere are you?
❑ How good are you at following up your promises?
❑ How consistent are you?
❑ Would you trust yourself to help if you were someone else?
❑ What resources do you have to deal with the situation?
❑ Can you trust in your skill to handle the situation?
❑ What similar situations have you been able to deal with in the past?

It is much easier to trust yourself when you have consistently shown the skills you need, or you believe that you can demonstrate them.

Trust in yourself comes from belief in your own resources, from experiences in the past where you showed these resources. These are your *reference experiences*. To be solid, these need to be grounded both on your own judgment and on feedback from others. Some people are internally referenced: they judge themselves according to their own values. They pay attention to their own subjective experience. It does not matter to them if people do not think they are good enough. Extremely internally referenced people do not pay attention to what other people think, and will not trust anything they have not personally tested.

Other people are more externally referenced: they need people to tell them that they are good, and then they will believe it.

Use both internal and external references. You need both to believe that you have the resources and to have feedback from others agreeing with you.

I would feel terrified if I were to drive around a racing circuit at over 100 miles an hour—it is dangerous. I have no experience in driving racing cars, but a racing car driver feels safe if they have successful experience of driving in similar situations. They know they have the skill, they have done it before. They trust in the mechanics who build and look after the car. They know what to do if they get into trouble on the track. They may feel the excitement of adrenaline, but very rarely do they feel fear.

Trust is the greatest resource against fear

❑ In the environment.
❑ In others.
❑ In yourself.

To trust another person, you need to see:

❑ Sincerity.
❑ Consistency.
❑ Congruence.
❑ Competence.

To trust completely you need to test the person to the limit. You want to see more strength than is needed in that particular situation.

Reference experiences

Reference experiences are past experiences that we pay attention to when we decide whom or what to trust. Of all the possible experiences that we could select, which ones count and which do not? Are all reference experiences the same?

NLP can provide answers with the "convincer" metaprogram pattern.

Some people will assume that they have the resources and skill they need with no reference experience, and go ahead anyway. This is an approach based on *faith*. The same people are likely to trust another person without any further check.

Other people need only to have been shown the skill on one prior occasion and that is enough for them. This is the *automatic* pattern. They feel that if they can do something once, then they can do it again, they don't need to keep proving it to themselves or other people.

Most people have a pattern that depends on the number of *examples*. They need several reference experiences before they trust in their own abilities. The number varies from two to ten. When I started as a trainer, I needed four successful trainings before I felt confident in my own ability to stand up in front of hundreds of people and talk about NLP. Some experiences count more than others. A training opportunity that started badly but where I triumphed in the end counted more for me than a training occasion that went well from beginning to end, because I needed more resources and flexibility than usual to turn it around. Flexibility is a higher-level resource, because when you are flexible you can change direction and get other resources, not just the ones you thought you needed when you started.

Some people have a *period of time* pattern. They need their reference experiences spread out over a certain time to convince them that they have the resources required. It could be days, weeks, or months, depending on the resource.

Others are never convinced. This is known as the *consistent* pattern. For them each time is like the first, they have to prove they have the resources. This makes it difficult to trust their abilities. The same people usually do not trust others either (unless they are very externally referenced).

People with the faith or automatic pattern may be overconfident and be mistaken about their abilities. It is usually better to develop the resource rather than assume it is there. Some people with the period of time or number of examples pattern may spend longer than they need in trusting themselves. The consistent pattern makes it difficult to trust your abilities however much you have developed them, but at least you will never be complacent.

Convincer metaprogram patterns

Automatic

Based on faith

Number of examples

Period of time

Consistent (never convinced)

Skill for freedom

Trusting your experience: What reference experiences count?

This exercise will help you see what evidence you need to know that you can trust yourself.

❑ Think of some resource that helped you change in a good way, or got you out of a dangerous situation in the past.

❑ How did you know that you had the resources you needed for that change?

— How important was other people's feedback?
— What experiences did you have that convinced you you had the resources you needed?
— Did you assume that you had them anyway and went ahead? (Faith)
— Was one past experience enough to convince you that you had the resource? (Automatic)
— Over what period of time did you have these experiences before you were convinced? (Period of time)

— How many experiences did you need before you were convinced? (Number of examples)

— Did you never really believe you had the resources, however much you had shown them in the past? (Consistent)

— Are you satisfied with the way you trust your experience? If you are not satisfied, what would you prefer to do?

Learning from experience

Regardless of how many times you show that you have a resource, one bad experience can loom large and can make you question your ability. It can cancel all the good experiences where you did show the resource.

This need not be a problem. Learn from that experience so that it will not happen again. When you know what went wrong, why it went wrong, and the difference between what you did then and what you did on the other occasions, then you can learn from the experience. Learning is impossible without mistakes, so never make the same mistake twice!

Here is a skill to learn from your mistakes, which is a variation of learning from the past (page 66).

Skill for freedom

Learning from experience

Sometimes a bad experience can make you doubt your abilities and be afraid to try again. The following pattern will turn this bad experience into a resource and learn from it. This pattern is not suitable for trauma or phobia.

1 Think back to the experience that made you doubt your skill or resource. Make sure that you see yourself (so that you are dissociated) in that situation as if on a television or movie screen.

2　Notice what was happening then, what other people did that contributed to the situation, and how it was impossible for you to control every aspect of the situation.

3　How might you avoid similar circumstances in the future?

4　Notice that there is a difference between having an ability (because you have expressed it before) and expressing it in this situation. What circumstances made it difficult for you? What were you trying to achieve? What did you want to happen?

5　With the benefit of hindsight, how should you have acted in order to achieve what you wanted?

6　Relive the incident again in your imagination the way you wanted it to happen. See yourself doing things differently, using the ability, and getting the result you wanted. Stay outside the experience; watch yourself acting in the situation on a mental screen.

7　When you are satisfied with that, imagine stepping into the situation and relive the incident in your imagination, the way you wanted. Be back there, seeing through your own eyes, acting the way you should have acted and getting the result you wanted. Then blank your mental screen.

8　Do step 7 at least seven times, reliving the event in the way you would have preferred it to happen, and then blanking out your mental screen at the end of each replay. Do it faster and faster each time.

9　Store this new experience you have just created as a mental video under "learning experiences."

10　Finally, think back to some experiences when you did have the ability. Go through them again associated—be inside the memory, seeing what you saw, hearing what you heard, and feel the satisfaction of being able to act in that resourceful way.

Understanding your reference experiences helps you to trust yourself.

The first reference experience

Suppose that you have no reference experience yet, or you have a consistent pattern when every time seems to be the first time. You need to create or assume a reference experience.

Here are some ways:

❏ Have faith in yourself. Faith is deeper than confidence. You need faith when you have no reference experience for the resources you need, but you go ahead anyway because you believe in yourself as part of something greater. You know that you are more than your skills or behavior. You feel the fear and do it anyway. Faith is often associated with religion, but it always goes with a feeling of connection with something greater than yourself, something more than your isolated ego.

❏ You can use a similar experience in the past as a reference experience if it is close enough to what you want.

❏ You can act as if you have the resource you need—you can express it in your behavior, even if you feel you do not have it.

❏ Find someone whom you trust and who believes in you. Ask them why they believe in you and what they have seen and heard that makes them think that you have the resources you need. Listen to what they say and see if this is enough to convince you.

❏ You can trick yourself or someone else can trick you.

This last method was how I learned to swim. When I was about six years old, I used to go to the swimming pool every week, although I could not swim yet. All of my friends could swim and they tried to reassure me that I would be able to. (In fact, I was not worried so much about swimming, I would have been happy just to float.) They would jump in and splash about and have a lot of fun. They would try to prove that I wouldn't sink if I kept air in my lungs. They told me it was easy and I should just do it. They held me up in the water, but as soon as they let go I would start to struggle and panic. I did not doubt what they said, I believed that they were sincere, but somehow I was afraid—afraid of the water, afraid that I was the one exception in the whole of the human race that would disprove the laws of physics. Surely I suffered from negative buoyancy and would sink whatever I did.

I used to play in the pool wearing a small inflatable lifejacket and would quite happily jump in and swim across out of my depth, confident that the jacket would support me. One day, I was at the pool and playing with my friends. I jumped in as usual and started swimming across the pool. When I got halfway across I suddenly realized that I was not wearing my lifejacket. This really was a sinking feeling. For one terrible moment, I struggled and started to go under, before realizing that I had made it halfway across the pool under my own steam and all I had to do was to keep on doing what had got me that far, and it would get me the rest of the way. It did. After that I had a reference experience and have enjoyed swimming ever since. Some skills such as swimming and riding a bicycle only need one reference experience.

Intuition

We can avoid most danger if we pay attention to our intuition. Intuition lets us know something without knowing how we know. It is not logical, because it does not come from the conscious mind, but it is not illogical. Our intuition has a reason; we just don't know what it is. A good intuition has a compelling urgency. But how can we tell a genuine intuition from our imagination? How can we develop a good intuitive sense?

First, intuition is not a gift for the lucky few, but a natural quality. We notice far more than we are aware of. We can feel how another person feels because emotions are contagious, we have empathy with others. All emotions are expressed in the body in facial expressions, muscle tensions, and altered breathing patterns that result in different voice tonality. When two people talk, you can see something called "motor mimicry." When one person smiles or frowns, the other will smile or frown back, even though those smiles or frowns may be for a fleeting fraction of a second. We mirror other people's expressions without noticing. This happens without our intention; we do it from infancy as a way of connecting with others and building rapport.

These unconscious responses can come to consciousness as an intuition about what another person is thinking or feeling, because our body is going through the same expressions and so we recognize them and link them to emotions.

Second position

We notice the slight changes in color, breathing, voice tone, and muscle tension of another person. We imagine what it would be like to take on those patterns. When we do this, we feel the same as they do; it gives us the same feeling because we are both human and our neurology works in the same way. We then get the intuition of what the other person is feeling. In NLP, this is called emotional second position.

The other kind of second position is cognitive second position. This is when you have an intuition of what the other person is thinking. The basis of intuition is to sharpen your skills of second position.

How do you experience your intuition?

For some people it is a feeling, usually in the pit of the stomach. We talk about "gut feelings" that we have at a deeper level than logic. You may have these feelings anywhere in your body. Have you ever had the experience of the hairs on the nape of your neck standing on end, or goose pimples on your arms for no apparent reason? This could also be your intuition.

For other people, intuition can be an internal voice, telling them to be careful. Sometimes it tells them not to trust someone. Trust is often based on intuition. Most people want to be trusted, and to appear trustworthy.

Intuition can save your life, and it can make the mundane world a more interesting and vibrant place.

Skill for freedom

Getting to know your intuition

Remember an occasion when you had an intuition about someone.

Make sure this intuition was:

❑ Accurate.
❑ Useful.
❑ Surprising because it was not obvious.

How did you experience it?

(If you cannot recall an occasion, imagine what it would be like. You can also do this exercise later when you have developed your intuition from some of the following exercises. Then you will have a real experience to use.)

What intuitions did you have about the person?

How did you become aware of those intuitions?

❑ Was it an internal voice?
❑ If so, where did the voice come from?
❑ How loud was it?
❑ What was the tone?
❑ Was it your voice or did it belong to someone else?
❑ How far away did it seem to be?
❑ Was there anything else you noticed about that voice?

Was it a feeling?

❑ If so, where was the feeling located in your body?
❑ How big was the feeling?
❑ How deeply inside your body did it seem to be?
❑ Where did it originate?
❑ What temperature was it—hot, warm, or cold?

❑ How intense was it?
❑ Was there anything else important about that feeling?

Was it an internal picture?

❑ If so, where was the picture located in your visual field?
❑ How far away did it seem to be?
❑ How bright was it?
❑ Was it black or white or colored?
❑ How intense was it?
❑ Was there anything else important about the picture?

This will help you to be aware of how your intuition comes to you, so you will be more familiar with it and know when it is trustworthy.

Allow your intuition

There are many ways to develop intuition. You pick up far more information than you are consciously aware of, so you are always having intuitions. Do not "try" to have intuitions; this will stop them. Intuition is like a shy friend who has to be coaxed into your house by making it a welcoming place. Therefore, the main way to develop intuition is not to block it. There are three enemies that will block intuition, one visual, one auditory, and one kinesthetic, and to each there is an antidote.

The three enemies of intuition

The *visual* enemy of intuition is foveal vision. How you use your eyes affects how you think. There is a spot in the center of the retina of each eye called the *fovea centralis*. It has the greatest concentration of cells (called cones), which are sensitive to color and bright light. Foveal vision is staring directly at an object; the image falls on the fovea. It engages the analytical conscious mind; it focuses directly on the object and does not see the space around it. Foveal vision is good for concentration and analysis.

The antidote is peripheral vision. This is when you let your field of vision expand to take in as much as possible without straining.

Athletes who use this type of vision call it "soft eyes." When you use peripheral vision, you engage the other type of cell in the eye, called rods. These are concentrated at the edges of the retina. They are sensitive to shades of light, speed, and movement. (If you want to cross the road, it is much easier to judge the speed and distance of approaching cars by looking out of the corner of your eye than by staring straight at them.)

Peripheral vision takes in information without trying. You cannot analyze it all, so you select unconsciously and this opens the door to intuition.

People who live in dangerous cities are more aware of their environment than most people. They see possible danger signals. They sometimes seem to have "eyes in the back of their head," like Andrea did when she noticed the two men who were following us in Rio.

Skill for freedom

Developing peripheral vision

Here is a short exercise to develop peripheral vision.

Stare intently at something in front of you. Look at it in detail.

Notice how the focus of your eyes affects the way you think.

Now, without moving your head, let your field of vision expand.

Be aware of what lies outside your central focus. Notice how opening your vision also seems to open your mind—there is space all around you, but you won't get anything from it unless you are aware of it.

Now focus back on the object in front of you, while keeping the sense of awareness of what lies on either side of it.

The *auditory* enemy of intuition is internal dialogue. When you are talking to yourself, you cannot hear sounds on the outside. Nearly everyone talks to themselves to some extent, it is a useful aspect of thinking, but because it uses words, it can block intuitions coming into consciousness in the form of words or sounds.

The antidote is simple. Just listen to what is going on in the outside world. Don't name it or try to understand it, simply listen. Listen to the sound of someone's voice as well as what they are saying. Also opening the peripheral vision quiets the internal dialogue and helps to relax the muscles of the face.

The *kinesthetic* enemy of intuition is unnecessary muscle tension. The antidote is relaxation. Because intuition comes from the ability to unconsciously take second position, to engage in motor mimicry, you need to have your own muscles relaxed to get these fleeting signals. The face is the most expressive part of the body This is where you get the most intuition about the other person's intentions through unconscious micro muscle movements that mimic the other person. A lot of tension can build up in the muscles around your jaw and your neck; begin by relaxing here. This will also help you to quiet your internal dialogue, because the inner voices usually synchronize with muscle movement in the throat and jaw.

Five ways to develop your intuition

There are many ways to develop intuition once you are aware of its enemies:

❏ First, people watching. From an early age, I had a low boredom threshold and found it impossible merely to sit somewhere without doing something to amuse myself. I would look at the people around me and make up a story about their lives. Who was the man sitting at the table next to mine? He could be an office worker having a clandestine lunch with his secretary. Arthur Conan Doyle made his detective Sherlock Holmes able to tell an enormous amount of information about someone's life and work just by observing them for a few seconds, to the amazement of his sidekick Dr. Watson. Sherlock Holmes was a fictional character, but the sort of information he picked up is available to everyone. So the next time you are in a restaurant or airport, indulge in a little people watching. What can you tell about them? Make up a story about their lives, where they were born and what sort of life they have. This is fun to do and will sharpen your powers of observation.

❏ Secondly, talk to children. Children are usually more open in what they say and body language than adults. As we grow older we learn to hide our feelings more expertly. It is easier to catch children's moods.

❏ The third way to develop intuition is to do more listening than talking. When you are talking you are attending to what you are saying; you are not open to how the other person is feeling and responding. When they are talking, concentrate on what they are saying and how they are saying it, rather than on what you are going to say next. The best way to listen deeply is to quiet your internal dialogue. When your inner voice is running, commenting on what is being said, judging yourself and the other person, getting ready with your reply before the other person has finished their sentence, there can be no real listening. Also, if your intuition manifests itself through an inner voice, it will not have a chance to get through with all the chatter going on.

❏ The fourth way is through your dreams. Dreams are a wonderful source of intuition because they are messages from your unconscious. Record your dreams for a week. Have a notebook beside your bed and as soon as you wake up, write down as much as you can remember. So many times we have interesting dreams and vow to remember them, only to discover that they disappear like early morning dew after waking with all the cares of the day pressing in for attention. When you have recorded your dreams, look at them later in the day at a quiet time. Do not leave it too long, because dreams reflect the preoccupations of the day, and may not be so relevant the next day. What could your dream mean? Guess; let your mind wander into all the things, people, and events that it reminds you of. A variant of this is before you go to sleep each night, have a question in mind. In the morning, think how your dreams during that night could be an answer to your question.

❏ A fifth way is to write "morning pages." Immediately after you get up, write a page of whatever comes into your mind. Write about how you feel, what you want to do that day, your hopes, dreams, regrets, and fears. You can write about anything. Do not censor (and it is usually not a good idea to show your morning pages to anyone else). Many professional writers do this to open their mind. First, your mind will be clearest in the morning after you wake, before the cares and responsibilities of the day have had a chance to get their claws into you. Secondly, if you write with no fixed agenda, the fleeting thoughts and intuitions have a chance to come to the surface. Your unconscious is like a friend, who will open up if you listen. Even good friends will not tell you what they think if you continually argue or ignore them. Morning writing builds rapport with your unconscious. It helps to balance your thinking. Morning pages are best written in longhand, to engage your kinesthetic sense. Also your handwriting is the unique way you have of expressing yourself and intuitions flow more readily to the paper than to the wordprocessor.

In everyday life, we often disregard intuition because we are afraid that it is wrong. We dismiss it, or want logical justifications. Never be afraid of your intuition being wrong. It is better to look a little stupid than to put yourself in danger by not paying attention to what your intuition is trying to tell you.

Here is a final skill to put together all the ideas on intuition.

Skill for freedom

Developing intuition

Pick a conversation that is not important. Maybe strike up a conversation with an acquaintance (safely!).

As you talk to the person, open your peripheral vision. Keep looking at them, but let your vision expand to take in as much as possible. You are not looking for something, you are just looking at the surroundings. It will not make you look vacant or stupid, don't worry.

Quieten your internal dialogue and just listen to what the person is saying. Listen to the sound of their voice. Listen to the silence behind their words. Often the most interesting things about conversations are not what people say, but what they do not say—what they leave out or skip over.

As you do this, just relax the muscles in your forehead and jaw and around your eyes.

- ❑ What intuitions do you get about that person?
- ❑ What sort of mood are they in?
- ❑ What emotions do you pick up?
- ❑ What do you think they are interested in?
- ❑ Are they worried?
- ❑ What do you think their relationships are like?
- ❑ What are they afraid of?
- ❑ What work do they do and what do they enjoy about it?

If it is appropriate, you can check some of these intuitions by asking a few questions.

This skill will develop your intuition—you will be safer, and a more responsive and sensitive person.

PART IV

Finding Freedom— Techniques to Overcome Your Fears

CHAPTER 15

The Value Behind the Fear

The last of the human freedoms is to choose one's attitude to any given set
of circumstances.
VIKTOR E. FRANKL

THIS FINAL PART IS ABOUT FREEDOM. Freedom has two different meanings.
The first is freedom *from*. That has been the emphasis of this book so
far—freedom from fears. The second is freedom *for*. When you free
yourself from unreal fear, what will you do? How will life be different?

We value our freedom and we have fought for it for many years:
the freedom not to be restrained by others, the freedom to live our
lives as we wish, the freedom to travel, to meet who we want, to enjoy
life. Freedom is the opposite of slavery, where we have to obey other
people for no reason except that they are stronger than us. We think
that the enemies of freedom are other people, coercing us to do
things we do not want to do. But what about internal coercions?
What about the fears that hold us captive, the fears that restrict our
lives? It is hard to locate the enemy, because they are part of us, but
they can restrict us more than an external enemy. This book will help
you beat the enemies of freedom that have set themselves up inside
you.

Every fear has a positive intention, in other words it is powered by
a value, something we treasure. There is always a value underlying our
fear. The value can be such things as status, self-respect, honesty, rep-
utation, safety, or freedom. When we have a possible loss, we are
afraid. We cannot lose something we do not have, so it must be something that we have already and that is important to us—it has value.

This chapter will explore how you can use these values to free
yourself from fears. We are adopting a martial arts approach to

freeing yourself from fears—using the adversary's own strength to beat them.

The value under the fear

Here is a simple example of how a value and a fear interact. Imagine this scenario. A teenage boy gets his first job. He works in an office and often goes to the staff restaurant for lunch. One day he is there with his mates and he sees a beautiful woman sitting at another table chatting with her friends. He likes what he sees. He makes a few discreet enquiries and finds out her name and the department where she works. It seems that she has just joined the firm and works in an office quite close to his. She is a little older than him.

The next day at lunch, she is there. He steals glances across to her table; she does not seem to notice and is having an animated discussion with her friends. The next day he resolves to go early to lunch and try to get to know her. His male hormones and 35,000 years of evolution are impelling him in her direction.

He spends the morning unable to concentrate on his work, wondering how to make the first move. Why? He feels a little afraid. He argues with himself that there is no risk, but the butterflies in his stomach tell him otherwise. Reason does not disperse them. Suppose she has a boyfriend? Suppose she ignores him? What if she laughs at him? And her friends join in? Suppose everyone in the canteen suddenly stops talking and looks at him? Suppose it gets onto the office grapevine and everybody knows? Suppose... Suppose... Suppose...

What is he afraid of? Rejection. Looking like a fool. Failure. But why is this so frightening? If it was not frightening, he would get up his courage, read some dating books, and go and say hello. The thought of rejection is enough to make his heart beat faster and the butterflies run amok in his stomach. The fear might stop him from trying to talk to her. If he has been rejected before in this situation, then it will be more difficult for him.

He may talk with a (male) friend and get some support and advice so that he feels better. The next day if he steps across the canteen floor toward her table, he will be in transition. He can't go back without loss of face, he is committed, and there she is in front of him, he needs to say something better than "Uh... Can I use your tomato sauce?"

Rejection is loss of self-esteem and self-esteem is very important. The very value that motivates him (together with his hormones) to approach her is the one that is threatened if he is rejected. This is what makes the risk seem a large one.

Self-esteem

Loss of self-esteem underlies a lot of fear. Self-esteem is an abstraction that is much used in psychology. Everyone has some intuitive idea about what it means. It is not something tangible we possess or put on, like a suit of clothes, but something we create from moment to moment. It is our valuation of our self-concept.

There are two important ideas here: values and self-concept. Your self-concept is how you think of yourself based on what you do, and what you do is influenced by your self-concept.

When you act in an honest way, you will have a self-concept of yourself as an honest person. If you value honesty, then every time you act in an honest way, you build your self-esteem. Every time you act dishonestly, you will lose some of your self-esteem, unless you can justify this with another value that is equally important in that moment. You are the one who decides what is honest and dishonest,

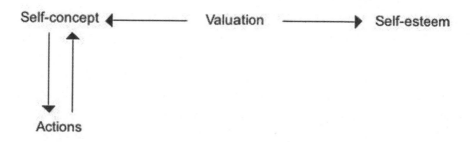

and your valuation of honest and dishonest acts depends on your culture, your experiences, and your upbringing.

Values act as a system: there is no overriding "top-dog" value that always wins when you make a decision. Your actions are determined by the interaction of your values depending on the context.

What erodes self-esteem is the gap between what you aspire to and what you do. Self-esteem is not fixed. It is how much you value yourself right now. When you do not act in accordance with your values, you lose self-esteem. When you act in harmony with your values, you build self-esteem. The values you incorporate in your self-concept are learned from your culture, environment, significant experiences, and significant adults, including your parents. Self-concept is also a social construct. It is difficult to be in a culture or an environment that defines as bad something that you value.

Suppose a man were brought up in a brutal environment where survival depended on being strong and exploiting others before they exploited you. He would value dishonesty and competitiveness and every time he behaved so, he would increase his self-esteem. He would feel good about being bad ("bad" as defined by others from other cultures with different values). Imagine this man having a Pygmalion-like conversion to a more civilized environment. The behavior that brought him self-esteem in the other environment would not be approved in the new environment and he would have a problem—those around him no longer respect his values. Either he would start to question his values and change them (which would be no bad thing), or he could stick to his guns and keep doing what he did before. He might be ostracized and lose his new friends, but he would be true to what he knows.

Self-esteem does not depend on being good; it depends on living your values, whatever they are. And I am not arguing that all values are equal, I do believe that some values are better than others.

The teenager wanting to meet the girl in our example values himself as a man and values his ability to attract women. He wants to talk to the woman, but he is in a difficult situation. His self-esteem may also depend on having the courage to approach her. Yet even if he summons up the courage to approach her, he may be rejected.

Rejection would shake those values, so rejection makes him afraid. The greatest loss is the loss of self—life, or self-concept. Remember that most people are loss averse. If the teenager is successful, then this maintains his self-esteem. It may not boost it very much, but rejection would definitely be a loss of self-esteem. He stands to lose more than he would gain. He does not know if he will be accepted. His friend may have no such qualms if his self-esteem is not injured by rejection.

The value of respect

Here is another example. I have a friend who values respect. She values respect from other people and she values respecting other people. Her self-esteem is increased when she gives respect to others and when others give her respect. A few months ago, we were both staying at a hotel in Rio de Janeiro and she went to ask for something from the hotel porter at the front desk. The porter was as rude as he could be without actually being downright insulting. He rolled his eyes, he turned away, and he sighed. He gave the Brazilian equivalent of a Gallic shrug that eloquently said how he felt: "Quit bothering me with your questions, you're a nuisance. If only this hotel did not have any customers to serve, everything would be OK." My friend gave up. She became angry, turned her back, and walked away. This porter did not respect her as either a person or a customer.

The next day, she wanted something else from the front desk, and the same porter was on duty. She confessed to me that she was afraid to go and ask. This was not because she was afraid of the porter as a person: he had simply been boorish, he was not an ogre, or likely to attack anyone. She was afraid that the porter would not respect her again, and this would make her feel more angry and upset. She could not help it, because respect was such an important value for her. Another person might have responded by getting angry. They would complain to the management and try to get the porter reprimanded. At the extreme case, in the culture of Los Angeles street gangs, "dissing" (disrespecting) someone can get you killed. Some people deal with this sort of situation by dividing themselves in two. They feel disrespected as a customer, but not as a person.

For my friend it was very important to be respected, not in a servile way, but with a modicum of common courtesy. To put herself in a situation where that value might not be respected made her afraid.

Fear of looking stupid

I have a personal example about values. Portuguese is the language of Brazil and living here, it is essential to speak Portuguese. I was learning Portuguese all the time in different ways: in formal lessons, from my own book study, and of course by listening and talking. It was very important to learn and speaking is the quickest way to learn. Yet, I found that I was reluctant to speak Portuguese. Why? I was afraid of looking stupid. I have always valued language and the ability to express myself well in words, and I was frightened of situations where I could not. I was afraid of other people thinking that I could not express myself, or of the embarrassment of saying something completely wrong.

Two values were causing the fear. The first was the value of being able to express myself. I did not want that to be questioned. Secondly, I did not want to appear stupid. Of course, there are many good reasons why these fears do not make sense. I can hardly expect to express myself well in a language I am learning. And people were not making fun of me when I made a mistake, but helping me. They did not think I was stupid.

To overcome this fear I did three things.

The first was to concentrate on the positive value of learning Portuguese.

The second was to change my value of not appearing stupid. This is an away-from value. It was important for me not to feel stupid. I changed this to the value of being intelligent. Trying out and learning a foreign language is intelligent.

Thirdly, I reframed mistakes as fun, and learning a language gave me carte blanche to say stupid things with little responsibility.

The next exercise will clarify how fear and values work together.

Skill for freedom

Transforming fear through values

1 Think of some situation in your life now where you want to do something but you feel afraid to act, although there is no physical danger to you or anyone else.

2 What is the value that is making you want to act? This is your *action value*. These questions can help to find it:

- ❑ Why do you want to act?
- ❑ What is important about acting in this way?
- ❑ What will acting in this way get for you?

Make sure you express this as a positive value, not as something you do not want.

3 How would going ahead express that value regardless of the result?

4 What is the value behind the fear? This is your *fear value*. The following questions can help to get to this value:

- ❑ What could you lose in that situation?
- ❑ What does that loss mean to you?
- ❑ If you feel you would lose self-respect or the respect of others, why would that be, what does it seem you would lack?
- ❑ What value would you not be living up to in your own eyes if you failed?

5 The fear value is often negative. If your answer is a negative value (i.e., it is important for you to avoid something), then what is the opposite positive value? For example, if it is important to you that you do not look weak and you are afraid of looking weak, then

strength is the opposite positive value. How would going ahead express strength regardless of the result?

6   Would failure to achieve what you want affect your action value, which is behind you wanting to act in the first place?

Fear of commitment

No book on fear would be complete without exploring fear of commitment. Many men and women want to commit themselves to another person, maybe by living with them, maybe through marriage, yet they are afraid. Often they procrastinate until their partner gets tired of waiting and leaves. Sometimes they flee as soon as the relationship starts to get more intense. Sometimes they keep the relationship cooler, knowing that they are missing something, but not knowing how to get over the fear.

The word "commitment" has three definitions in my dictionary:

❏ The state or quality of being dedicated to a cause or policy.
❏ A pledge or undertaking.
❏ An obligation that restricts freedom of action.

It is the third meaning that sparks the fear. We are afraid of losing freedom: freedom to do what we want, to please ourselves and not someone else.

Different words about commitment also have many negative meanings. For example, "committal" is used to describe sending someone to prison or mental hospital. We take about "committing a crime." The word group has many bad anchors.

Commitment is an abstract noun. No one is afraid of an abstraction. What they are afraid of is committing themselves, of taking action that they think might lose them something of value.

Skill for freedom

What does commitment mean to you?

Think of yourself committing to another person.

What feelings do you get?

What picture do you see in your imagination?

What sounds do you hear?

Is there an internal voice?

Is committing an all-or-nothing state or do you have various levels of committing?

What previous experiences do you have of committing yourself to another person and what happened?

Many social factors reinforce fear of commitment. There is a culture of individualism in the United States and Europe—the "sovereign individual." We are proud to be the masters of our own lives. This is especially true for women, who for most of history have been told what to do by men. Fear of commitment has been traditionally a man's province, but this is no longer true. It affects both men and women.

Films and television have given us many unrealistic expectations about love and commitment. Love is often portrayed as an irresistible force that sweeps you away, so people expect to be swept away. If they are not, they question what is happening. Maybe they are not in love? Love is shown as something that happens to us, instead of something that we work on, something that grows when we make an effort to understand and trust the other person. Outside of soap operas, committing is as much an act of will as an emotion.

People often see commitment as an all-or-nothing state. Either they are completely committed, or they are not. It has to be one or the other. Commitment is not like that, we can commit ourselves gradually; it is a journey rather than a fixed point of arrival. Commitment has a lot in common with trust.

Freedom has become a very important value in society, and when we commit, it seems like we lose our freedom. This is the loss-averse way of looking at it. We also gain much more, but these gains do not seem as real as the loss.

Commitment is a risk. We need to trust our partner, because we are making available the most precious thing we have—ourselves.

What is the value behind this fear?
The value is being liked or loved for ourselves. When we commit to someone we open ourselves out to them. We let them see us without a mask. Suppose they do not like what they see? Does this make us unlikeable? No. If one person does not like us, that does not mean that we are unlikeable. It means that *they* do not like us. Another person may.

The fear of being unlovable can make people afraid of committing themselves. It is too big a risk, and they may not like themselves, so how could anyone else like them? However, by not committing themselves, they do not open up to anyone else, no other person can see them and so they can never get an answer to the question "Am I loveable?" They can never lay the question to rest. Also, by not committing they do not get to know themselves deeply through another person's eyes.

This is not a book about relationships and commitment, but here is a skill that can help you explore fear of commitment.

Skill for freedom

Exploring commitment

To deal with a fear of commitment, you need to explore these questions:

What are you afraid will happen?

What is the value behind the fear?

What are you afraid of losing if you committed yourself?

Do you feel you have to commit yourself all at once?

What would you gain if you committed yourself?

What would it be like to have committed yourself?

What do you think you would lose?

"Hell is other people," said the existentialist philosopher Jean-Paul Sartre. To this I would reply, "So is Heaven." We are formed by and through relationships with others. We cannot be alone, because we define ourselves in our actions with others. We need to connect and commit to other people to be fully ourselves.

Commitment may seem like losing yourself, but it is the only way to truly find yourself.

CHAPTER 16

Dealing with Fear in the Body

Change and pain are part of life but suffering is optional.

THE FEELING OF FEAR, BOTH AUTHENTIC AND UNREAL, is unmistakeable. The fear response, orchestrated by the amygdala, leads to feelings that are like no other. It can make us freeze or panic. The fear response directs blood away from the brain, therefore when we are frightened we do not think so clearly. We need some way to deal with the feeling so that we can feel more resourceful, and take action.

Controlling your feeling of fear

What can we do to control the physiological feeling of fear? To begin to answer this question, do this small experiment.

Sit in a chair and relax your body. Make sure that you relax the muscles in your forehead and the back of your neck. Breathe in and out deeply and slowly a few times.

Now try to feel afraid. Think of something that might normally make you afraid. Make sure that you stay relaxed and breathe in a slow and measured way.

Can you feel fearful?

The odds are that you cannot. When we relax, we are not able to feel fear, worry, or anxiety to anything like the normal extent. Emotions are a loop between body and mind. The mind creates fearful pictures. This makes us feel tense and changes our breathing. Our brain reacts to the mental images as if they are real. The tension and breathing pattern back up the feeling of fear. A vicious circle is set up. When we break the link between the anxious thoughts and the usual physio-logical response, we cannot feel afraid in the same way. Our brain is trying, but our body says: "What danger?" When we relax the body, fear cannot get a foothold.

Thinking strategy

Fear

Physiology of fear

We can use NLP to stop the thinking strategy, or to change the physiology. Then we can think clearly about what to do.

There are three main ways to relax and control the feeling of fear. Before you start, rate your fear on a scale of one to ten, where one is slight fright and ten is absolute terror. Then as you use some of the following processes, rate your fear again after a few minutes. It should be lower. Keep doing the process until the fear is gone or down to a reasonable level.

Controlling fear through breathing

Breathing is the key to relaxation. Changing your breathing pattern helps to make you feel relaxed. Quick, shallow breathing changes the acidic level of the blood and makes you feel more anxious, even when there is nothing to feel anxious about. "Take a good deep breath" is advice that many people give to help you be calm, but this is only half the story. If you take many good deep breaths too quickly, you will hyperventilate and this will make you feel panicky. To feel calm, you need to concentrate on the *out* breath.

To feel more relaxed and calm, breathe in slowly, for at least a count of three. Hold your breath for a moment and breathe out for twice as long as you took to breathe in. This will calm you for both unreal and authentic fear.

When you can control your breathing in this way, you will find that what was anxiety turns into a feeling akin to excitement. Excitement gives you energy to meet the challenge. Anxiety makes you want to run away from it.

This is also the reason laughter is such a good resource: it changes your breathing, distracts you, and releases beta-endorphins—natural chemicals that make you feel good. Laughing at your fears does work.

Controlling fear through feeling

This seems a paradox. However, you cannot will your feelings away; when you try to do this, it usually makes them worse. Just feel the pure feeling. The feeling is unpleasant because you are not getting into the pure feeling, you are thinking of it as fear and trying to escape it.

To control fear in this way, feel it deeply, simply as a feeling. Go through the exercise on page 146, and really explore the submodalities of what you are feeling. Pinpoint the exact place you are feeling it. Explore how hot or cold it is, how intense, how deep in your body. Don't have any thoughts about it; don't try to get rid of it. Just feel exactly what is there.

One tip to help you: look down. Looking down helps you contact your feelings. Where you place your eyes is important to your thinking. Looking up helps you think in pictures. Looking to the side helps you think in sounds.

Once you have the pure feeling, then you can play some games with it. Move it around. If it is in the middle of your abdomen, move it up into your chest, then down to your belly, then maybe into your knee or your big toe. What is it like to have a frightened knee? See how far you can control the feeling by moving it. When you move it, see if it stays there.

Controlling fear through relaxation

The best way to control anxiety is by relaxing your body and mind. Many things people do to "relax" like watching television are not relaxing at all. Your body may be slumped in the chair, but the television has control of your mind, you are open to all the images it sends. These may add to your stress.

When you do any relaxation exercise, pay particular attention to your forehead, neck, and shoulders. It is easy for tension to settle in a furrowed brow, tight shoulders, and stiff neck. As we get older, muscle tension draws lines on our face where we are habitually tense. We carry muscle tension in our body without noticing because we are used to it.

Some years ago, I took lessons in both the Alexander technique and the Feldenkreis method. Both are means of being more aware of the body and using it in the most effective, efficient, and graceful way. I remember in one lesson, my teacher asked me to stand up absolutely straight. I did so. She asked me if I was sure I was standing straight. I said yes, it felt like I was straight. Then she brought a full-length mirror and showed me how I was really standing. I was amazed to see I was leaning to my left. I could see that in the mirror. The feedback I had from my body was mistaken. When I thought I was standing straight, I was leaning to the left. So I changed my posture so I could see I was standing straight. It felt like I was leaning to my right, even though I could see it was straight in the mirror. I had the habit of leaning to the left and had done it for so long that it felt correct.

You may think your neck is relaxed, but in fact you do not feel the tension because you are used to it. You can do three things to help you relax more fully.

Before you relax a part of the body, tense it as fully as you can. Get a sense of what it is like when it is very tense. Then relax as fully as possible. By tensing first, you will be able to relax more because you will be able to notice the difference more clearly.

Secondly, feel the muscle with your hand. Feel the back of your neck and massage it gently. Feel your forehead and smooth out the furrows.

Thirdly, take a relaxing massage whenever you can. At the end, be aware how your body feels. Then when you relax by yourself, you will have a better idea of what it feels like when you are fully relaxed.

Proper relaxation helps to control stress and anxiety. Also, by building in a time for relaxation every day, you help the body to relax and relieve the symptoms of stress. Each day's relaxation helps to lessen the load on the body. Of course, you can never relax every muscle in your body. You need some tension, otherwise you would collapse like a jelly.

There are many excellent relaxation books and tapes on the market (see References, page 245). Here is a simple relaxation exercise to do every day for a few minutes that will make a big difference to your stress level.

Skill for freedom

Relaxation exercise

❏ Lie down in a quiet place where you will not be disturbed for a quarter of an hour at least. Close your eyes. Become aware of your body, starting from the feet and working up, or from the head and working down. Be aware not just of the limbs and muscles and the outside of the body, but also the inside—the organs and muscles that are working all the time to keep you alive and well.

❏ Notice what feels good in your body. Also, notice those places that do not feel good, either because they are painful or there is a feeling of malaise. Simple awareness will help. Do this for at least five minutes. Do not try to change anything, just notice what arises.

❏ Breathe deeply into your abdomen and let your lungs fill from the bottom upward. Feel that you are filling your whole body with the vital force in the air.

❏ Hold your breath for a moment and imagine charging the air within you with vitality from all of your body that feels good. Let all the good feeling from your body pass into the air.

❏ Exhale, and as you do so, imagine pushing the charged vitality of the air to every part of your body and feel it invigorating all your body. Let all the pain and stress in your body pass in the air you are exhaling into the surroundings and be lost.

You can supplement this relaxation with another skill—witnessing. Fear has no power unless you identify with it, in other words think that it is an essential part of who you are. Witnessing is a way of disidentifying with the fear. You see the fear as something you have and separate from the real you. The essential you is not touched by fear. The real you is never frightened. The real you simply feels. As soon as you separate yourself from the fear and witness it, it loses its power.

The following skill is the most useful one in the whole book. It is not just a short-term process for controlling fear when you feel frightened. It is a spiritual exercise that helps you separate the real you from all the conflicting feelings and attachments that you have to everyday life. It is a form of meditation and if you do it every day, you will be less identified with fear and anxiety and less stressed. It will help you to center yourself. It will give you more resources to absorb the stress that life sends your way. It will help and nourish you at a deep level, whatever fears you may have.

Skill for freedom

Witnessing

Relax and say the following to yourself. The words do have to be exact.

"I have a body, but I am not my body.
I can feel and see my body, so I cannot be my body."

Pause a moment and let this sink in.

"My body may be tired, anxious, sick, or healthy, but this is nothing to do with the real me. I have a body and I am not my body."

Pause.

"I have wants, but I am not my wants.
I can know what I want; I am more than what I can know.
I can be aware of my desires, but they do not touch the real me.
I have wants and I am not my wants."

Pause.

"I have emotions, but I am not my emotions.
I feel my emotions and what I can feel and sense cannot be the true me.
Emotions come and go but do not affect the real me.
I have emotions, and I am not my emotions."

Pause.

"I have thoughts, but I am not my thoughts.
I am aware of my thoughts, so I cannot be them.
Thoughts come and go but do not affect the real me.
I have thoughts, and I am not my thoughts."

Pause.

"Who am I really?"

CHAPTER 17

Dealing with Fear
in the Mind

Courage is resistance to fear, mastery of fear—not absence of fear.
MARK TWAIN

NLP PROPOSES THAT WE LEARN UNREAL FEARS and then they are constantly triggered by anchors. Every time you change your thinking and use your resources, you weaken the strategy and help to unlearn the fear.

How does this work in practice?

I have a personal example that will illustrate many of the ideas in this book. When I was writing the book, I trained on some NLP courses in Rome. When the training was over, Andrea and I had allowed ourselves a couple of days to experience the sights, sounds, tastes, and smells of the Eternal City. The Spanish Steps, the Coliseum, and many wonderful churches vied for our attention. Rome is unique. One moment you can be walking down a dirty, narrow street flanked by graffiti-encrusted buildings. It seems as if you are in an insalubrious suburb of a third-world sprawl. Suddenly you emerge into a beautiful piazza, with dazzling examples of bygone architecture.

How could we visit Rome without going to the heart of Christendom? We had to visit St. Peter's Church. The square in front of the Basilica is spacious and beautiful. We arrived mid-morning, just missing the Pope's weekly address. The chairs were still laid out in the square. We went straight to St. Peter's Church to see as much of it as possible in the time we had.

The church is a work of art in itself, quite apart from the sumptuous pictures, frescoes, and statues that surprise you from every corner. The enormous dome that forms the top of the church was built in 1590 and is a miracle of engineering. From the floor of the church, we stared up into the dome with its magnificent art—the details were lost high above us. We joined the queue to ascend into the dome, where we heard every language except Italian.

When we got to the head of the queue there were two ways to go: with the elevator and without it. It was cheaper to go by foot and we wanted the exercise, so we elected to climb the stairs, despite a warning notice telling us that there were over 300 of them. We set off enthusiastically. The stairs went up in a wide spiral and with plenty of space to begin with. People kept their distance from each other and we circled slowly upward; the climb was a pleasure for the first 150 steps. Then the stairs narrowed and the spiral became tighter.

We emerged from the steps into a gallery at the top of the church, and still the dome towered above us. Looking down gave me vertigo, so I stayed away from the edge and we set off to climb the next set of steps. These were much narrower and went up in an even tighter circle than the first set and the treads became narrower and narrower.

If that were not bad enough, there were several largish windows looking out onto the city, and we were very high by this time. The wall pressed me on the inside. Outside, the view was of either an immense sky or the ground below. It was like being in a dungeon on top of a cliff. Also, the climb had made me a little breathless. It was a perfect environment to induce agoraphobia and claustrophobia simultaneously. I did feel uncomfortable, even though I do not suffer from either of those.

I continued climbing and hoped that we would emerge at the top of the dome soon. I was curious why I was feeling like this. The feeling made no sense. I was perfectly safe.

What was I imagining? That I was climbing a spire with nothing between me and a sheer drop on one side.

This was like a nightmare from *The Lord of the Rings*, like climbing a stair that got smaller and smaller as you went further and further up. I also had a mental picture of the stairs getting smaller and smaller and tighter and tighter until they became so small and cramped that I could not get any further—a kind of birth trauma fantasy. In another disaster scenario, the stairs collapsed and I was trapped. In all of these pictures, I was associated, looking out through my own eyes and being there rather than seeing myself in these predicaments.

Using my resources

I had to do something. I dissociated from the pictures and *saw* myself in those situations rather than *being* in them. That made me feel better immediately. From this new point of view, these imaginings were ridiculous. This church had been standing for hundreds of years and it was not going to collapse now. Thousands of people had ascended these stairs without mishap. The next thing I did was to think of something to make me feel better. I thought back to earlier that day when we had bought some Venetian glass in one of the small shops off St. Peter's Square. The glass was beautiful and I imagined putting it on the table in our apartment. I felt much better thinking about our apartment than thinking about the narrow winding stairs.

Next, I thought about my experience in airplanes. I have flown hundreds of times and it has never made me nervous. Here I had my feet on the ground (even though the ground was high up). If flying did not frighten me, why should this?

As I thought about this, I heard someone a little further down slip and swear loudly in English. I went to see what had happened. A man had turned his ankle on one of the slippery steps and had sat down to rest. I asked him if he was all right. His face was pale, even in the gloom. He said that he was OK and he had a couple of friends to help him, so I left him to recover.

I kept climbing, pushing myself forward and concentrating on putting one foot in front of the other. Andrea came next to me and put her hand on my arm and asked me if I was OK. I said yes, and I felt better.

I also did not want to show other people that I was afraid. I value being the sort of person who is fit, can climb, and has little trouble with heights. And I wanted to reach the top of the dome because I wanted to know what was there.

We came at last to the top. It was worth it. The sight was marvelous. The beauty banished my fears.

Summary of resources

When I reviewed this experience, I thought of the strategies I had used to deal with the situation.

❑ The first resource was *curiosity*. I was interested in my fear, so I could view my feelings from a distance and observe them dispassionately. I could witness my fear rather than be inside it.

❑ The second resource was *reason*. I told myself that what was happening was not reasonable. This can help with mild fears, but it is difficult to talk yourself out of a strong emotion. Secondly, this strategy uses the auditory system (talking to yourself) when the fear is usually created in the visual system (pictures of disaster). As long as you believe what you see in your imagination, self-talk will not help.

❑ The third resource was discovering the *strategy* I was using to create my fear. I was making frightening pictures in my mind and associating into them. When I dissociated from the picture and saw myself in it, it was no longer something that was happening to me, so I lost the feeling of fear. I was an observer and I could see it as unreal.

❑ The fourth resource was to think of something to *change* my emotional state—something that made me feel good and secure, in this case the Venetian glass.

❑ The fifth resource was *counterexample*. I found an experience similar to what was happening where I felt OK (traveling by airplane). I had flown without fear, so why should I feel frightened now?

❑ The sixth resource was a *distraction*. An outside shock interrupted my thoughts. When the man shouted, I was brought back to the real world from my scary mountainside fantasies.

❑ The seventh resource was paying attention to *someone else's* troubles. This again brought me out of my mental world and focused me on what was happening. My concern for the other man made me forget for a while about my own fear.

❑ The eighth resource was my *identity*. I do not see myself as the sort of person who is frightened in that situation.

❑ The ninth resource was to *avoid* the bad consequences of giving into my fear. I did not want to feel wounded pride, so I continued upward. I did not want to show other people that I was afraid.

❑ The last resource was wanting to get to my *goal*. I wanted to see what was at the top of the dome.

All of these were useful resources. I did not give in to the fear. If I had, I could have strengthened the fear of heights and enclosed spaces and it would have been more difficult to challenge it next time.

Strategies for relieving fears and anxieties

1 *Curiosity*—become curious about your fear. What is happening?

2 *Reason*—tell yourself that the fear does not make sense.

3 *Mental strategy*—find out how you are creating the fear by becoming aware of your mental pictures. First dissociate from the pictures and evaluate them objectively. Then apply the cognitive analysis.

4 *Changing your emotional state*—by thinking of something else.

5 *Counterexample*—do you have a similar experience when you did not feel afraid? What made the difference then? How can you use that in the present context?

6 *Distraction*—pay attention to something on the outside that has nothing to do with the fearful situation.

7 *Concern for others*—pay attention to someone else's problem.

8 *Identity*—do you see yourself as the sort of person who would be frightened in this situation?

9 *Avoidance*—avoid the bad feeling of giving in to the fear.

10 *Your goal*—think of what you want to achieve and be determined to get it.

All these strategies will work providing you take a first essential step: you want to do something about your fear.

Types of resources

These resources fall into five categories.

Changing your emotional state

Curiosity is a very strong resource state. You can get curious about your fear. As you get interested in your emotional state, this helps in two ways. First, the emotion of curiosity starts to displace the emotion of fear. Secondly, as we discussed in Chapter 2, awareness of a feeling helps to disperse it. When you are curious, you can look at your fear as something separate from you instead, something you have and not something you are. When you are curious about something, you can overcome your fear.

I changed my emotional state by thinking of something else that made me feel good. This is using an NLP resource anchor and is a powerful way to combat fear.

If you do not have a resource anchor, here is how to create one.

Skill for freedom

Creating a resource anchor

1 Decide on the exact state you want to feel. For example, secure, calm, or relaxed.

2 Think of a time in your life when you had that quality. That state is a resource from the past that you will bring to the present with an anchor.

When you have identified a time, imagine yourself back then, associate into the memory, and experience it again as fully as you can. If you cannot remember a time, then put yourself in a calm, relaxed, and secure state either by imagining such a situation or with relaxation exercises (see page 212). By doing this, you will automatically be associated in the state in the present moment.

3   Set an anchor for that state as follows.

While you are associated in the state:

❑ Pick an auditory anchor—a word or phrase that links strongly with that state, for example "I am safe."
❑ Pick a visual anchor—either something mundane that you know you will see in a fearful situation, or a visual memory, or a symbol.
❑ Pick a kinesthetic anchor—a natural movement that you can do easily. Breathing out slowly would be a good choice.

4   Come out of the state and be aware of your surroundings.

5   Test the anchor you have made.

Say the phrase to yourself, see the visual cue, or if that is impossible imagine it In your mind, and make the movement that you decided on.

Notice how you feel safe and relaxed.

If the anchor does not work, go back to Step 3. Associate as fully as you can into that state, be fully back in that time, hearing what you heard, seeing what you saw, feeling what you felt. Make that state as strong as possible. Then set your anchors again.

When you have tested the anchor and have found it works—practice! Resource anchors are useless if you forget to use them. Practice your anchor at least 20 times. The more you practice, the more it will become automatic.

If you want the anchor to help you with a particular fear, for example fear of flying, then mentally rehearse getting on an airplane and using the anchor. This will help you remember when you next board an airplane.

Using a resource anchor is a mental strategy. It is a sequence of pictures, sounds, and feelings. The outcome is to make you feel better. When you create a resource anchor you are relearning. You use a new mental strategy to cancel the original one that was creating the fear, and a new anchor to replace the trigger that made you feel afraid.

Distraction

This is called a *break state* in NLP terms. A break state is anything that interrupts the emotion you are feeling by taking your attention. While you cannot do an effective break state on yourself (how do you surprise yourself?), you can get someone to talk to you or tell you a joke.

You can break state in three different ways:

❑ Visual, by seeing something interesting or surprising.
❑ Auditory, by hearing a sudden sound or music.
❑ Kinesthetic, by a touch.

You can use break states on other people when they are frightened or in another unresourceful state.

Self-talk

You can reason with yourself. Tell yourself that it makes no sense to be frightened. Use a reassuring tone of voice. A scary Stephen King type of internal dialogue can frighten you even more. First, use a soft, relaxing tone of voice. Secondly, use positive statements. When you say to yourself "Don't be frightened," you are focusing on being frightened. It is better to say "I can feel calm" or "Feel calm!" (in a calming voice tone, of course). Make the voice tone match the sort of feeling you are trying to have. Sometimes it is just helpful to say repeatedly "Calm" or "Relax" in a calming voice tone. This acts as a kind of hypnotic mantra and if it works, you can use it as a resource anchor.

Values

Values are powerful against fear. When other people are in trouble, especially those you care about, then you suddenly forget your fear to help them. Afterward, looking back on what you did, you may hardly believe what you did.

Secondly, there is a sense of achievement. Many people who face real danger, such as climbers and explorers, can conquer their fear because they want to know the answer; they want to reach their goal because it is important to them.

Last, you may start to wonder if you are the kind of person who would be frightened and value your lack of fear.

Mental strategy

In the church I used the principles that we have already discussed in Chapter 6. I found the pictures and sounds I was imagining and dissociated from them. I substituted my own pictures and sounds and also paid attention to people on the outside. When you pay attention to pictures and sounds on the outside, then you have less attention to give to the pictures and sounds on the inside. It is your attention that provides them with power.

Freedom *from* fear is a lot to do with what you choose to pay attention *to*.

CHAPTER 18

Freedom From Social Anxiety

Society, my dear, is like salt water, good to swim in but hard to swallow.
ARTHUR STRINGER

EMOTIONAL FREEDOM MEANS that you will see all the myriad social anxieties for what they are—a choice; *one* way to live, not *the* way to live. These social "under-thoughts" generate a host of specific fears, which cannot be conquered fully without tackling the root causes—the social assumptions behind them.

The Hydra of social fears

The specific fears are like the heads of a mythical monster called the Hydra. According to Greek legend, the Hydra lived in the swamps near the ancient city of Lernea. It looked like a dragon with nine heads. To kill this monster, you had to cut off the heads, but every

time you cut off one head, two more would grow in its place. One of the nine heads could not be harmed by any weapon. The Hydra would come from the swamp regularly and terrify the countryside, eating people and cattle, nine at a time.

Eventually the monster came to the attention of the hero Hercules, as one of his 12 labors to atone for killing his family. Hercules' original strategy was to cut off the Hydra's heads, but he soon realized that this would only make things worse, so he got his friend Iolaus to cauterize the neck every time he cut off a head and this stopped the head from growing again. After a heroic battle, Hercules managed in the end to cut off all the heads but one. This last head could not be killed, so Hercules crushed it with his club, ripped it off, buried it, and put a large stone on top.

Unreal fears are like the Hydra's heads, a violent metaphor but a very fitting one. They need to be cut, but also you have to stop the thinking—the social under-thoughts that generate the fear in the first place. This cauterizes the fear so that it cannot grow again.

Beheading the Hydra

This book is full of stylish NLP swordplay to cut off the head of your particular fear. All the moves have three things in common:

❑ Recognize the unreal fear and what it does.
❑ Recognize and retain the positive intention.
❑ Change the strategy that creates the fear.

What are the social under-thoughts that generate so many fears? What gives rise to the Hydra's heads?

❑ The first head is generated by *blame*. When you blame others or yourself, you will be afraid of the consequences of some undefined punishment or being found out. The fire to cauterize this neck is *responsibility*. Take responsibility for your own actions and change what you can. Many people and events have contributed to the situation. No one is to blame.

❏ The second head is generated by *information overload*. When you have too much information you cannot get the information you need to appraise a situation and know if there is anything to fear. You may be afraid that you have missed something and in the end opt to be "better safe than sorry." The fire for this neck is *precision questions* that come from clear and precise goals.

❏ The third head is *time pressure*. Time pressure makes deadlines that cause anxiety and worry. The fire you need is *perspective*. You choose how you see time. When you see your timeline in perspective you can plan your work so that whatever strategy you use, the deadline will be motivating rather than fear provoking.

❏ The fourth head is *fear of the future*. The future does not exist yet; we create it from what we do now. All fear of the future is unreal. The fire is an *action plan* from a clear goal. You do what you can and get help where you need it. Many problems cannot be solved alone: think globally—act locally.

❏ The fifth head is *too much choice*. Too many options are confusing and can make you afraid of missing something, and lead to a kind of paralysis. The fire is *balance*. When you balance your tendencies for maximizing and satisfying, you will make good choices. Good enough is good enough. Remember the rule of three: narrow your choices down to the best three available.

❏ The sixth head is *change*. You cannot stop change, but you can *manage the transition* that gives changes their power to frighten you, which is the fire you need here.

❏ The seventh head is an excessive *focus on achievement*. Fear of failure follows quickly behind. The best fire to apply is a *focus on being*. Achievement is about doing and it tends to define you in terms of what you do. Who are you really? Much more than your achievements. All your achievements are generated from you and you are greater than anything you can do. When you focus on being you will be more in the present moment and get happiness from the journey toward your goal, not just from arriving at the destination.

❑ The eighth head is generated by *limiting beliefs*. When you believe you are less than you are, you will be afraid to try, because you fear failure. Limiting beliefs make you less than you are. *Humility* is the fire to apply. Your beliefs are not the truth, they can be wrong. All you know is that you have not reached your limits. Paradoxically, humility will allow you to discover that you are greater than you think.

❑ *Loss* is the ninth head. Perhaps this is the head that can never be killed completely, only buried. Loss is part of life. Some things we choose to leave, others are ripped away from us. Sometimes despite everything, we suffer loss. We lose something that is dear to us and it was not our choice.

Life in the present moment

We cannot be conquered by loss, because we are more than anything that we can have, or think, or possess, or mourn. We cannot control events, but we can control our reaction to them. We cannot control the outside world, but we can have choices in our inner world. We cannot control other people, but we can wish them well and help them to be the best they can be. We can never know ourselves completely, so we can never control ourselves either, because we are more than we can know. We can witness everything that happens, the joys, pain, love, and hate, and know that everything we see out there has its shadow inside us, that we are part of the world and we cannot make ourselves separate from it.

Buddhists have it right. If you are not attached to anything, you cannot lose anything, but you will still feel the pain of loss. Do not deny the pain—it means that you care and that you are alive.

CHAPTER 19

Emotional Freedom: Here and Now

Learn from yesterday, live for today, hope for tomorrow.
ALBERT EINSTEIN

WE ALL WANT EMOTIONAL FREEDOM—to live life free from unwanted fear. Primary fear will always be there to protect us, but many people live their lives within fear: fear of risk, fear of failure, fear of authority, fear of loss. They live inside a barrier. When we live most of our life *inside* fear, we will be unhappy.

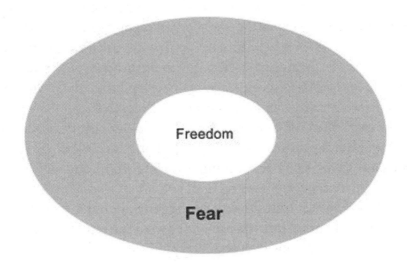

Freedom

Fear

Life within fear

Instead, live outside the fears so that they do not restrict you.

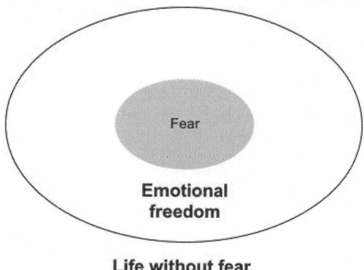

Life without fear

When you live most of your life *outside* fear, you live a life of emotional freedom. With NLP you have choice about what you feel. You need a full range of feelings, even the so-called bad ones—grief, sadness, and anger. They all have energy and purpose. You can decide to stop some, and you can feel fully the ones you choose to feel.

You will never be free of authentic fear, nor would you want to be. Authentic fear remains as an instinct, a biological reaction, keeping you safe and giving you the extra energy to fight or flee.

Emotional freedom means no corrosive worrying. You will not have any more sleepless nights worrying about family, money, work, bills to pay, or anything else. All these are important, but worrying is not the way to deal with them. Instead, you will have a goal and an action plan. You don't know whether it will work, but you will have done your best and there is nothing more to do at that moment.

Emotional freedom means that you are free from unreal fear and you can discover your true talents. Fear stops you from attempting so many wonderful things.

229

What would you do if you knew that you could not fail?

How important are those things?

Could fear of failure be stopping you right now?

Opening doors

Emotional freedom gives you more possibilities. Many doors open to you that fear had closed. You never know what is possible if you don't try. Freedom from fear gives you a much more realistic view of yourself. You will know yourself better. You will know your limits, because you will not be afraid to test them. You will know what you like and what you do not like. You will be more authentic. When you are more authentic, you will also be able to commit to another person if you want to—*you* will decide.

Emotional freedom lets you see the positive intention behind the fears and take care of that in a way that is less stressful, less limiting, and more joyful.

Courage

The way to conquer all fear is to take action. When someone acts bravely, we say that they have courage. But is courage something they "have"? Courage is not a mysterious, ether-like quality that some people possess and others do not. Courage is how we describe the actions people take to face their fear and to conquer it. Courage is action. Courage takes you through your fear and out the other side.

One thing I have learned in dangerous cities such as Rio is that if you think you are being followed, stop and look into the follower's eyes. See them and let them know you have seen them. You may fear them, but you face them anyway. This keeps you safer than pretending not to notice, or ignoring the possible danger.

Courage helps you feel the fear and do it anyway. There is a nice moment in the film *The Three Kings*. This is centered around a group of American soldiers fighting in Iraq. Three of them are out in the desert and have to make a decision whether to go back for their captured comrade. One of the soldiers is very afraid. The second soldier, played by George Clooney, says, "You don't get courage to help you do something you are afraid of. You start doing it and then you get the courage."

Courage is the link between fear and action. Our imagination, one of our greatest gifts, comes like all great gifts with a double edge. We can imagine wonderful futures and be inspired. Equally, we can imagine awful futures and be afraid. Courage helps us to imagine the wonderful futures and deal with the awful ones. Although the title of this book is about fear, it is really a book about courage.

Finally, there is a skill in Part I of this book (page 33): "What are you afraid of?" Here is a final exercise to close that circle. When you have done it, compare your results to those in the first exercise and notice the changes. Try it. What are you afraid of?

Skill for freedom

What were you afraid of?

What have you been afraid of in your life that you are no longer afraid of?

Make a list on the lefthand side of a sheet of paper of everything you can remember being afraid of but are no longer.

On the righthand side of the paper list why you are no longer afraid of these things.

Write down any significant event that might have helped you lose that fear.

How is that different from your answers on page 33?

Thinking about Thinking with NLP

IN THIS BOOK, WE HAVE EXPLORED FEAR and various ways of feeling fear through mental pictures, sounds, and feelings.

NLP proposes that we think with internal images (visual), sounds (auditory), feelings (kinesthetic), smells (olfactory), and tastes (gustatory). These are the internal counterparts of our senses that we use on the outside to explore the world. They are known as *representational systems* in NLP literature. The world is "presented" to our senses, and then we "re-present" the world to ourselves in our minds using these internal senses. This internal representation is powerful and determines how we react, regardless of the "real" experience. Therefore NLP seeks to change how we think about our experience.

What we see, hear, and feel in the outside world has smaller components, for example distance and direction. Sounds can be loud or soft, pictures can be bright or dark. Feelings can be hot or cold. These smaller components or qualities of our internal senses are known in NLP terms as *submodalities*. All our internal pictures can be described in terms of visual submodalities, all internal sounds by auditory submodalities, all internal feelings by kinesthetic submodalities. These submodalities can be a critical part of the way we think about our experience. Association and dissociation, for example, is a very important submodality and I have used it in this book in many strategies to combat fears.

Here a list of the main submodalities, many of which are used in exercises in this book. For a complete description of NLP thinking and submodalities, see *The NLP Work Book*, listed in the bibliography.

Visual submodalities

❏ *Associated/dissociated*—seen through own eyes or looking on at self.
❏ *Color*—color or black and white.
❏ *Boundary*—framed or unbounded.
❏ *Depth*—two- or three-dimensional.
❏ *Location*—left or right, up or down.
❏ *Distance*—far away or near.
❏ *Brightness*—bright or dark.
❏ *Contrast*—well defined or poorly defined.
❏ *Focus*—clear or blurred.
❏ *Movement*—still, smooth, or jerky.
❏ *Speed*—fast or slow.
❏ *Number*—single screen, split screen, or multiple images.
❏ *Size*—large or small.

Auditory submodalities

❏ *Verbal or nonverbal*—words or sounds.
❏ *Direction*—stereo or mono.
❏ *Volume*—loud or soft.
❏ *Tone*—soft or harsh.
❏ *Timbre*—fullness of sound.
❏ *Location*—up, down, left, or right.
❏ *Distance*—close or far.
❏ *Duration*—continuous or discontinuous.
❏ *Speed*—fast or slow.
❏ *Clarity*—clear or muffled.
❏ *Pitch*—high or low.

Kinesthetic submodalities

The kinesthetic representational system covers:

- Vestibular (balance).
- Proprioceptive (body awareness).
- Tactile (touch).

Feelings may also be:

- Primary (feeling in the body).
- Meta (feeling about something else).

The following kinesthetic submodalities apply to all of these categories:

- *Location*—where in the body.
- *Intensity*—high or low.
- *Pressure*—hard or soft.
- *Extent*—large or small.
- *Texture*—rough or smooth.
- *Weight*—light or heavy.
- *Temperature*—hot or cold.
- *Duration*—long or short, continuous or discontinuous.
- *Shape*—regularity.
- *Movement*—still or moving.

Olfactory and gustatory submodalities

Some basic kinesthetic submodalities can be applied to smells and tastes:

- *Location*—where in the body.
- *Intensity*—high or low.

- ❏ *Extent*—large or small.
- ❏ *Temperature*—hot or cold.
- ❏ *Duration*—long or short, continuous or discontinuous.
- ❏ *Movement*—still or moving.
- ❏ *Quality*—sharp or sweet.

Summary of Skills for Freedom

References

Introduction
For September 11th archives, see: www.nytimes.com

Chapter 1 What Is Fear?
For the phobia pattern see Joseph O'Connor (2000) *The NLP Work Book*, Thorsons, p. 107.

Chapter 2 Fear—Friend or Foe?
For information on learned helplessness, see C. Peterson, S. Maier, & M.E.P. Seligman (1993) *Learned Helplessness: A Theory for the Age of Personal Control*, Oxford University Press.

For a general consideration of social fears, see Joanna Bourke (2005) *Fear: A Cultural History*, Virago.

Chapter 3 Learning and Unlearning Fear
A useful resource for children's fears is at
http://www.childdevelopmentinfo.com/disorders/fears.htm
Six Flags Magic Mountain Rollercoaster:
www.sixflags.com/parks/magicmountain/index.asp

Chapter 4 The Language of Fear
The Bene Gesserit litany is from Frank Herbert (1971) *Dune*, Simon & Schuster.

Chapter 5 Fear in Time
T. Cottle (1967) "The circles test, an investigation of perception of temporal relatedness and dominance," *Journal of Projective Technique and Personality Assessments*, No. 31, pp 58–71.

For NLP material on PTSD (post-traumatic stress disorder) see Dr. D. Muss (1991) *The Trauma Trap*, Doubleday; R. Bolstad (2002) *RESOLVE: A New Model of Therapy*, Crown House.

For more details on stress and worry from the NLP viewpoint see Joseph O'Connor & Ian McDermott (1997) *NLP and Health*, Thorsons.

Chapter 6 Common Fears that Hold Us Hostage

The anxiety and panic internet resource:
http://www.algy.com/anxiety/relax.html

Perceptual positions first came to NLP through the work of John Grinder and Judith de Lozier, see John Grinder & Judith De Lozier (1992) *Turtles All the Way Down*, Grinder De Lozier.

Hong Kong Two International Finance Centre:
www.skyscraperpicture.com/2ifc.htm

Chapter 7 Unquiet Times and Turbulent Minds

Information on W.H. Auden: www.audensociety.org/

Forbes magazine: www.forbes.com/forbes

Mercer quality of life survey:
www.mercerhr.com/pressrelease/details.jhtml/dynamic/
idContent/1128760

Information about São Paulo:
http://www.embratur.gov.br/en/cidade/ver.asp?servicoId=63&id=386
http://anhembi.terra.com.br/turismo/eng/

For ideas on the area of influence and area of concern and the link to health, see J. Marx (1980) "Coronary artery spasms and heart disease," *Science*, No. 208, pp 1127–30.

Stress management resources: http://stress.about.com/cs/relaxation/

Chapter 8 Social Fears

For an excellent book on time management see Mark Forster (1999) *How to Get Everything Done*, Hodder and Stoughton.

Googlewhacking: www.googlewhack.com/

Research on happiness, see P. Brickman (1975) "Adaptation level determinants of satisfaction with equal or unequal outcome distributions in skill and change situations," *Journal of Personality and Social Psychology*, No. 32, pp 191–8.

Choice, maximizers, and satisfiers, see David G. Myers of Hope College and Robert E Lane of Yale University, www.sciam.com, April 2004.

Chapter 9 The Pressure to Achieve: The Price of Perfectionism

To understand cultural differences see Fons Trompenaars (1997) *Riding the Waves of Culture*, Nicholas Brealey Publishing.

For an interesting overview of motivation through achievement see http://www.cultsock.ndirect.co.uk/MUHome/cshtml/psy/motivat.html

For Maxwell's ideas on blame see http://www.amazon.com/exec/obidos/ASIN/0785274308/early-torise-20/

For a great book performance anxiety see Eloise Ristad (1976) *A Soprano on Her Head*, Real People Press.

For public speaking and presentation skills see Joseph O'Connor & John Seymour (1994) *Training with NLP*, Thorsons; Robert L. Jolles (2000) *How to Run Seminars and Workshops*, McGraw-Hill; Andy Bradbury (2000) *Successful Presentation Skills*, Kogan Page.

Chapter 10 Dealing with Change: The Uncertain Future

For metaprogram patterns see Shelle Rose Charvet (1997) *Words that Change Minds*, Kendall-Hunt.

For a more general treatment of change see Paul Watslawick (1993) *Change*, WW Norton; James Claiborn (1998) *The Habit Change Workbook*, Simon and Schuster.

A good guide to Brazil: http://www.lonelyplanet.com/destinations/south_america/brazil/

Jonathan Swift (1995) *Gulliver's Travels*, Signet Classic.

For coaching in transition see Joseph O'Connor & Andrea Lages (2004) *Coaching with NLP*, Thorsons.

Chapter 11 Fear as a Sign to Take Action

For information on the Darwin awards, see www.darwinawards.com

Chapter 12 How We Assess Safety and Risk

For the best overview of risk, see Peter L Bernstein (1996) *Against the Gods*, John Wiley & Sons.

Daniel Kahneman & Amos Tversky (1984) "Choices, values and frames," *American Psychologist*, Vol. 39, No. 4, pp 342–7.

Chapter 13 Acting on Fear: When to Heed the Warning

For research on rapport see William Condon (1982) "Cultural Microrhythms," in M Davis (ed.), *Interaction Rhythms: Periodicity in Communicative Behavior*, Human Sciences Press; Howard Friedman & Ronald Riggio (1981) "The effect of individual differences in nonverbal expressiveness on transmission of emotion," *Journal of Nonverbal Behaviour*, Vol. 6.

For cross-cultural body language see Desmond Morris (1994) *Body Talk: A World Guide to Gestures*, Jonathon Cape.

For personal safety and danger signs see Gavin de Becker (1997) *The Gift of Fear*, Little Brown.

Chapter 14 Trust and Intuition: Your Two Guides

For metaprogram patterns on trust see Shelle Rose Charvet (1997) *Words that Change Minds*, Kendall-Hunt.

For an interesting article on intuition, see http://www.fastcompany.com/online/38/klein.html

Chapter 15 The Value Behind the Fear

The best approach to self-esteem in NLP is Steve Andreas (2002) *Transforming Your Self: Reinventing Who You Want to Be*, Real People Press.

Chapter 16 Dealing with Fear in the Body

For details of the Alexander technique see
www.Alexandertechnique.com
Society of the teachers of the Alexander technique:
www.stat.org.uk
For witnessing and spirituality see Ken Wilber (1998) *The Essential Ken Wilber*, Shambhala; Thomas Leonard & Michael Murphy (1995) *The Life We Are Given*, Penguin.
For relaxation resources see Martha Davis (1997) *The Relaxation and Stress Reduction Workbook*, HarperCollins.
For a comprehensive list of relaxation CDs and tapes, see
http://www.relaxation.clara.net/

Chapter 17 Dealing with Fear in the Mind

About St. Peter's Church, Rome:
http://www.roma2000.it/zschpiet.html
http://www.twenj.com/rometour1.htm

Chapter 18 Freedom From Social Anxiety

The Hydra: http://www.pantheon.org/articles/h/hydra.html
For an interesting approach to emotional freedom, see Peter Levine (1997) *Waking the Tiger*, North Atlantic Books.

Chapter 19 Emotional Freedom: Here and Now

Read Ken Wilber (1991) *Grace and Grit*, Newleaf Publishing.

Bibliography

There are also other books listed in the References.

Andreas, Steve (2002) *Transforming Your Self*, Real People Press.
Bassett, Lucinda (1997) *From Panic to Power*, Harper Perennial.
Beck, Don & Cowan, Christopher (1996) *Spiral Dynamics*, Blackwell.
Becker, Gavin de (1997) *The Gift of Fear*, Bloomsbury.
Bernstein, Peter L. (1996) *Against the Gods: The Remarkable Story of Risk*, John Wiley & Sons.
Bolstad, R. (2002) *RESOLVE: A New Model of Therapy*, Crown House.
Bourke, Joanna (2005) *Fear: A Cultural History*, Virago.
Bourne, Edmund (1999) *Anxiety and Phobia Workbook*, New Harbinger Publications.
King, Serge (1990) *Urban Shaman*, Simon & Schuster.
Miller, Alice (1991) *Thou Shalt Not Be Aware*, Dutton.
Morris, Desmond (1995) *Bodytalk*, Crown.
Murphy, Michael (1995) *The Life We Are Given*, Penguin.
O'Connor, Joseph (2001) *The NLP Work Book*, Thorsons.
O'Connor, Joseph & Lages, Andrea (2004) *Coaching with NLP: How to Be a Master Coach*, Thorsons.
Peurifoy, Rameau (1995) *Anxiety, Phobias and Panic*, Warner Books.
Ristad, Eloise (1976) *A Soprano on Her Head*, Real People Press.
Rose Charvet, Shelle (1997) *Words that Change Minds*, Kendall-Hunt.
Schwartz, Barry (2004) *The Paradox of Choice: Why More Is Less*, HarperCollins.
Swami Nichilananda (2000) *The Principal Upanishads*, Dover.
Trompenaars, Fons (1997) *Riding the Waves of Culture*, Nicholas Brealey Publishing.
Wilber, Ken (1998) *The Essential Ken Wilber*, Shambhala.
Wilber, Ken (2000) *A Theory of Everything*, Shambhala.

About the Author

Joseph O'Connor

Joseph O'Connor is an internationally recognized author, trainer, executive coach, and consultant. He is a certified NLP trainer and a leading author in the field of leadership and systems thinking. He is the author of 16 books, which have been translated into 25 languages. His first book, *Introducing NLP*, is an international bestseller and has been established as the basic introductory text in NLP for over 14 years.

Joseph is in demand internationally as a trainer and consultant and was the first European trainer to give NLP seminars in Chile, where he presented NLP to a special conference attended by CEOs and members of the Chilean Senate, including a Presidential candidate. He has trained in Europe, North and South America, Asia, and New Zealand. He was awarded the medal of the Singapore National Community Leadership Institute for his work in training and consultancy in 1996.

His consultancy clients have included BT, UNIDO, BA, and HP Invent.

He lives in São Paulo, Brazil.

Contact Joseph at joseph@lambentdobrasil.com.

Lambent do Brasil

Lambent do Brasil was founded by Joseph O'Connor and Andrea Lages and is based in São Paulo, Brazil. The company specializes in providing the best resources in coaching, consultancy, and NLP training at every level, to develop individuals and companies.

Lambent do Brasil are founders of the Brazilian Association of Coaching and the Mexican Association of Coaching. They also supplied the majority of the training on the first National Coaching Register training in the UK, leading to a postgraduate degree in executive coaching from Derby University.

They also give the International Coaching certification training.

See www.lambentdobrasil.com or contact info@lambentdobrasil.com.

International Coaching Community (ICC)

The International Coaching Community is a group of trained and qualified coaches who have passed successfully through the International Coaching Certification training. There are currently over 600 coaches in 23 countries.

The ICC was founded by Joseph O'Connor and Andrea Lages. The Community has a shared commitment to quality, ethics, and high standards in coaching.

For details see www.internationalcoachingcommunity.com or contact info@internationalcoachingcommunity.com.